Contemporary Issues in Mediation

Volume 9

Related Titles by the Singapore International Mediation Institute

Contemporary Issues in Mediation Volume 1
ISBN: 978-981-3108-35-6
ISBN: 978-981-3108-36-3 (pbk)

Contemporary Issues in Mediation Volume 2
ISBN: 978-981-3225-63-3

Contemporary Issues in Mediation Volume 3
ISBN: 978-981-3270-81-7

Contemporary Issues in Mediation Volume 4
ISBN: 978-981-120-911-6

Contemporary Issues in Mediation Volume 5
ISBN: 978-981-122-052-4

Contemporary Issues in Mediation Volume 6
ISBN: 978-981-124-142-0

Contemporary Issues in Mediation Volume 7
ISBN: 978-981-12-6871-7

Contemporary Issues in Mediation Volume 8
ISBN: 978-981-12-8524-0

Contemporary Issues in Mediation

Volume 9

Joel Lee
Singapore International Mediation Institute, Singapore &
National University of Singapore, Singapore

Marcus Lim
Lupl, Singapore

with Muhammad Syazwan Bin Ramli

SIMI
SINGAPORE INTERNATIONAL MEDIATION INSTITUTE

World Scientific

Published by

World Scientific Publishing Co. Pte. Ltd.

5 Toh Tuck Link, Singapore 596224

USA office: 27 Warren Street, Suite 401-402, Hackensack, NJ 07601

UK office: 57 Shelton Street, Covent Garden, London WC2H 9HE

Library of Congress Cataloging-in-Publication Data
Names: Lee, Joel, editor. | Lim, Marcus, editor.
Title: Contemporary issues in mediation (v. 1) / Edited by Joel Lee
(Singapore International Mediation Institute, Singapore),
Marcus Lim (Singapore International Mediation Institute, Singapore).
Description: Hackensack, New Jersey : World Scientific, 2016.
Identifiers: LCCN 2016004240| ISBN 9789813108356 (hardcover : alk. paper) |
ISBN 9789813108363 (pbk.)
Subjects: LCSH: Dispute resolution (Law) | Mediation. | Dispute resolution (Law)--Singapore. |
Mediation--Singapore.
Classification: LCC K2390 .C667 2016 | DDC 347/.09--dc23
LC record available at http://lccn.loc.gov/2016004240

Contemporary issues in mediation (v. 9)
ISBN 9789819801251
ISBN 9789819801268 (eBook)
ISBN 9789819801275 (mBook)

British Library Cataloguing-in-Publication Data
A catalogue record for this book is available from the British Library.

For any available supplementary material, please visit
https://www.worldscientific.com/worldscibooks/10.1142/14053#t=suppl

Desk Editors: Soundararajan Raghuraman/Kura Sunaina

Typeset by Stallion Press
Email: enquiries@stallionpress.com

"This edition of *Contemporary Issues in Mediation* continues the strong tradition of thought leadership by SIMI. The range of articles showcase each writer's awareness of how mediation can be applied to and make an impact on a wide range of disputes, as well as how mediation processes can be impacted through Game Theory and Artificial Intelligence. The articles bear testament to the reality that there are generations of new talent in mediation that are coming on-stream, who will go on to shape a more collaborative approach to dispute resolution at all levels and thus help to heal this fractured world. Congratulations to SIMI for Volume 9 and I commend this handy publication to everyone who believes in the peaceful resolution of disputes".

Francis Goh
IMI & SIMI Certified Mediator
IMI Certified Mediation Advocate

"I am delighted to commend this outstanding compendium of articles which explore a rich tapestry of mediation practices and topics across a variety of crucial areas. This collection not only showcases the intellectual rigour and creativity of its contributors but also delves deeply into the intricate processes of mediation in such niche areas like human rights and victim-offender mediation (which *ex facie* do not appear to be suitable for mediation), as well as novel aspects of mediator professional development, such as through the adoption of Artificial Intelligence and a trauma-informed approach to mediation.

Each article stands as a testament to the authors' dedication, insightful analysis, and commitment to advancing the field of mediation. This compilation is an invaluable resource for professionals, academics, and anyone interested in the transformative power of mediation (and the underlying professional skills that mediators bring) in resolving conflicts and fostering understanding in diverse contexts".

A. J. Jawad
Advocate & Mediator
SIMI Accredited Mediator (Level 3)

Dedication

(5 June 1948–14 August 2024)

To Michael Leathes, A Visionary and A Giant in Mediation.
May his light continue to live on in our work and students.

https://doi.org/10.1142/9789819801268_fmatter

Contents

https://doi.org/10.1142/9789819801268_fmatter

Foreword for the Series

William Ury

A young man was hiking through the woods. He came to a clearing and sat on a rock to rest. As he ate his lunch, he noticed an old man moving through the clearing in a very deliberate way. The man would walk a specific number of steps, poke a hole in the ground with his walking stick, drop something in, and then repeat the process. Curious, the young man approached the old man and asked him what he was doing.

> The old man replied, "Well, I'm planting trees."
> "But why?" the young man asked.
> "When I was younger," the old man said, "this entire land was filled with trees. But over time, many trees had been cut down.
> I come here every day to plant trees."
> Fascinated, the young man asked, "How long have you been doing this?"
> "Forty years" was the matter-of-fact reply.
> "Forty years!" exclaimed the young man.
> "Yup," the old man replied. Gesturing to a grove of young trees in the distance, he said with some pride, "I planted those 10 years ago."
> The young man was incredulous. "That's great but these trees will take a long time to grow! And, if you will pardon me saying so, you may not live long enough to see the seeds you are planting today grow into trees!"
> "This is true," said the old man. "I have lived long enough to see some of the fruits of my labour. But the seeds I plant today are not for me, but for you."

It has now been just about 40 years since I had the privilege of embarking on the adventure of teaching and practicing in the field of negotiation and mediation. During that time, I have had the joy of learning from and working with many highly talented and skilled individuals in academia, law, business, and diplomacy. In those early days, there was very little scholarly writing in this area. After all, the field was relatively new and viewed by many with caution, if not outright scepticism.

Over the years, I have been gratified to watch the field of mediation grow considerably. Today, practitioners, teachers, and researchers can be found in every part of the world. The teaching, practice, and scholarship of negotiation and mediation constitute a dynamic system in which each contributes to the others. New tools and frameworks have been developed as a result of research, taught to practitioners, and then tested and refined in the field, which in turn has informed further research. This interplay between theory and practice has been vital in developing new insights and methods.

Yet the field of negotiation and mediation is still young. As we look back on the progress, we might be satisfied with the seeds we have planted which have sprouted into trees. Yet, as the concepts and practices spread around the world, we have a responsibility to ensure that future generations will be able to build on all that has been achieved. We must continue to plant seeds, not for ourselves, but for those to come.

This is why this book project by the Singapore International Mediation Institute is such a timely endeavour worthy of support. It is said that a journey of a thousand miles begins with a single step. The Singapore International Mediation Institute is taking that first step to inspire the youth of today and encourage them to engage in scholarship about mediation. It provides them with the platform and the opportunity to plant seeds for the benefit and enjoyment of future generations.

As the first of its kind in Singapore, I look forward to seeing this book series not only continue to flourish but also show the way forward through innovative and thought-provoking work.

I take this opportunity to wish you much success in getting to yes!

William Ury
Co-founder, Harvard Negotiation Project
Co-author, Getting to Yes
31 May 2016

https://doi.org/10.1142/9789819801268_fmatter

About the Editors

Joel Lee is a Professor at the Faculty of Law at the National University of Singapore. Joel co-pioneered the teaching of Negotiation and Mediation in Singapore Universities and has played a significant role in furthering the development of mediation in Singapore, not just in education but also in practice. A graduate of Victoria University of Wellington and Harvard Law School, Joel is a partner with CMP-Cambridge (USA) and a principal mediator with the Singapore Mediation Centre.

Joel was a member of the International Mediation Institute's Independent Standards Commission and Intercultural Taskforce and was also a key member of the Ministry of Law's Working Group on International Commercial Mediation. Joel is presently the founding Chair of the Board of the Singapore International Mediation Institute. He is also a certified trainer of Neuro-Linguistic Programming (NLP).

Joel has taught overseas at the University of Copenhagen (Denmark), University of Law, Economics and Science of Aix-Marseille (Aix-en-Provence France), and Anglia Law School (UK). He is the co-editor and co-author of *An Asian Perspective on Mediation* and the *Singapore Mediation Handbook*, and the general editor of the *Asian Journal on Mediation*. In 2011, Joel was awarded the Outstanding Educator Award, which is the National University of Singapore's highest teaching award. Joel was also awarded Singapore's Public Service Medal in 2023 for his work in promoting mediation.

Marcus Lim is the Director (APAC) of Lupl. Lupl is an open industry platform for legal matters that brings together people, conversations, documents, data, and knowledge, providing real-time 360-degree visibility and control for legal matters.

Prior to joining Lupl, Marcus was the first executive director, and later CEO, of the Singapore International Mediation Institute (SIMI), where he spearheaded many initiatives in growing the organisation into an internationally recognised and credible brand for mediation standards.

He is the Adjunct Assistant Professor for Negotiation and Mediation Workshops at the Faculty of Law, National University of Singapore, and was the coordinator for both courses in 2017. A graduate of the prestigious Law and Business Double Degree programme at the National University of Singapore, he is a consultant with CMP-Cambridge (USA). He is certified in the Thomas–Kilmann Instrument for Conflict and Change Management. Marcus is an SIMI-certified mediator, an associate mediator with the Singapore Mediation Centre, and a court-appointed volunteer mediator for the Small Claims Tribunal at the State Courts. Prior to joining SIMI, Marcus practiced at Rajah & Tann LLP's Competition and Technology, Media and Telecommunications Practice Group.

Marcus has extensive experience conducting negotiation and mediation training for the staff and management of government organisations as well as multinational corporations across a diverse range of sectors, such as finance, retail, real estate, IT, education, and healthcare.

Muhammad Syazwan Bin Ramli is a recent graduate of the Faculty of Law at the National University of Singapore, where he undertook courses in Mediation and Negotiation. During his undergraduate days, Syazwan was a seasoned participant in the alternative dispute resolution (ADR) competition circuit, representing NUS in notable international ADR competitions, such as the 18th ICC International Commercial Mediation Competition 2023 (ICC Paris) held in France, where he and his team won an award for Distinction in Teamwork between Counsel and Client and placed 6th worldwide. Syazwan has also clinched top awards in other ADR competitions, such as the CDRC A&G Inter-Varsity Cup 2023, the University of Central Florida Conciliator Mediation Tournament 2022, and International Mediation Singapore (IMSG) 2021. Since graduating, Syazwan has continued to serve as a coach for NUS Law's Collaborative Dispute Resolution Club, helping develop the negotiation and mediation skills of current law students.

https://doi.org/10.1142/9789819801268_fmatter

Editors' Note

It has been four years since the ratification of the Singapore Convention on Mediation ("SCM"). Since then, mediation has continued to gain traction worldwide, with the SCM continuing to serve as a testament to its pivotal role in shaping global dispute resolution practices. In 2024 alone, Japan, Nigeria, and Sri Lanka enacted legislation for the SCM to enter into force, reflecting the increasingly global acceptance of mediation.

As we continue to witness the transformative impact of the SCM on the global mediation landscape, Volume 9 of *Contemporary Issues In Mediation* (CIIM) presents a collection of ten diverse essays that reflect the applicability and importance of mediation and its development in various regional and international contexts. From exploring domestic issues in Singapore, such as using behavioural economics to enhance the resolution of disputes between neighbours (Li Kelun) and the applicability of victim–offender mediation in Singapore's criminal justice system (Chan Wayde), to more international perspectives, such as the exploration of opportunities for the strengthening of mediation practice in Russia (Natalia Kharitonova), it is clear that there is great latitude for the practice of mediation to be moulded in order to meet the needs of any given society. It is also clear that mediation can transcend diverse sociocultural settings, providing a framework to constructively navigate and address regional and international issues such as human rights violations in Asia (Joy Tan). These discussions are key to ensuring that mediation remains relevant as an essential facet of dispute resolution in societies around the world.

Another key theme of this volume is the interdisciplinary nature of mediation. Indeed, while legal knowledge remains crucial in mediation discourse, for instance in addressing unsettled legal issues such as the interpretation of Article 5(1) of the SCM (Jeriel Teo Sheng Wei), this volume contains essays that display how the practice of mediation can be enhanced with an understanding and combination of different fields of knowledge. These diverse fields include areas such as **education** and the development of mediation pedagogy through student competitions (Muhammad Syazwan Bin Ramli), **technology** and the use of artificial intelligence (Tristan Koh Ly Wey), **applied mathematics and game theory** in augmenting decision-making in mediation (Kyna Chew Qing Xuan), **social work** and the potential for a trauma-informed approach to mediation (Sebastian Hoe Wee Kiat), and even **behavioural science** in providing a greater understanding of the role of negative emotions and their utility to facilitating productive mediation (Erin Shan Liu). These contributions not only offer fresh insights into but also demonstrate the potential for cross-disciplinary collaboration towards a more holistic development of mediation in an increasingly connected world.

Volume 9 of CIIM encapsulates the dynamic and global nature of contemporary mediation. It serves as both a scholarly contribution and a practical guide for mediation advocates, mediators, educators, and policy-makers, highlighting the universal applicability and importance of mediation in fostering peaceful and constructive conflict resolution across the globe. We hope this collection inspires further dialogue and innovation, contributing to an enduring development of mediation worldwide.

As always, this publication would not have been possible without the support and effort of many people. We would like to take this opportunity to express our heartfelt thanks to the following people:

- Our wonderful families, for their unending patience and love;
- Mr. Muhammad Syazwan Bin Ramli, for his dedicated and invaluable professional assistance to the editorial team;
- Mr. William Ury, for writing the foreword for the series;
- Members of SIMI's board, past and present, for their unwavering support for the project (Ms. Charlene Chang, Professor Nadja Alexander, Mr. Poon Hong Yuen, Mr. Han Kok Juan, Mr. Calvin Chang, Ms. Josephine Hadikusumo, Mr. Michael Leathes, and Ms. Irena Vanenkova);
- The Singapore Ministry of Law, for continuing to support our work;
- The National University of Singapore Faculty of Law, for being a stalwart supporter of SIMI's operations;
- Our publishers, the World Scientific Publishing Company, for their patience and guidance in bringing another volume to publication; and

- Our students (past and present) from the National University of Singapore Faculty of Law, the Singapore Management University Yong Pung How School of Law, the Singapore University of Social Sciences School of Law, and from all over the world, who have always been an inspiration for our work.

Last but not least, we would like to thank you, the reader, for supporting SIMI and this book. We hope that this project continues to inspire you in your work, whatever field it may be, to find collaborative solutions in resolving your disputes.

Joel Lee and Marcus Lim
Singapore
10 August 2024

https://doi.org/10.1142/9789819801268_fmatter

About the CIIM Essay Competition

As part of SIMI's (Singapore International Mediation Institute) mission to promote awareness and interest in mediation, SIMI regularly organises an essay competition to help promote mediation academia among undergraduates and students in tertiary institutions. Submissions are welcome from students not only pursuing studies in law but also other disciplines. Selected entries will be featured in an annual edition of the *Contemporary Issues in Mediation*, with attractive prizes for some of the best submissions.

About SIMI

The Singapore International Mediation Institute (SIMI) was incorporated on 15 July 2014 as a non-profit organisation supported by the Ministry of Law. SIMI is a subsidiary of the National University of Singapore (NUS) and is housed at the NUS Faculty of Law.

SIMI is headed by an international Board of Directors with representatives from both mediation practitioners and corporate users of mediation, to further its mission to (1) set and achieve high mediation standards through the professionalisation of mediation; (2) promote understanding and inspire the use of mediation; (3) stimulate and facilitate the development and growth of mediation through research and innovation; and (4) foster a strong mediation community in Asia by engaging stakeholders in discussion, events, and outreach activities.

https://doi.org/10.1142/9789819801268_0001

Chapter 1

Mediation in Addressing Human Rights Violations in Asia

Tan Joy

I. Introduction

As an alternative dispute resolution process bringing together parties in conflict to discuss issues at hand and work together towards resolution, mediation has played a critical role in addressing and resolving human rights violations in various countries. Mediation is a powerful tool to address and acknowledge the harm caused by human rights violations and to promote reconciliation between victims and perpetrators. Mediation also functions as an accessible alternative or complementary dispute resolution mechanism in countries that face a combination of capacity, time and cost, and social and cultural constraints that may limit public access to formal legal services and it facilitates access to justice for the poor, women, and other marginalised communities.

As such, countries moving out of a period of armed conflict or civil war have often established mediation processes to address human rights violations committed during that period. However, such processes have mixed results and are at best only partially effective, often being criticised for not addressing all parties responsible or not doing enough for victims' rights, especially in countries in Asia.

In this chapter, the value and role of mediation in addressing human rights violations in and between various countries including India, Pakistan, Indonesia, Malaysia, the Philippines, and Thailand will be analysed. Building upon the experience of these countries, a recommendation is provided that the translation and implementation of mediation processes to address human rights violations within the Asian context is best facilitated through partnership with government and community-based actors and done in consultation with perpetrators, victims, and civil society.

II. Mediation in Addressing Asian Human Rights Violations

A. *Value of mediation in Asian contexts*

It should be stated from the outset that mediation as a method of alternative dispute resolution is not foreign to Asian contexts. As Asian cultures tend to situate the individual within the community and value social harmony, face-saving, and the collective good, it is said that Asian culture favours informal, non-confrontational methods of mediation and arbitration over formal legal systems. Litigation or public confrontation can be seen as damaging to personal and collective reputation. Although far from perfect, mediation offers many advantages that fit what Asian cultures value. Mediation allows parties to save face, fully participate in the proceedings, and shape the ultimate solution through a faster and cheaper process allowing for a more particularised justice with both sides feeling they have received their due. The process of mediation can help to build trust, facilitate dialogue between parties, and generate creative solutions that address the root causes of the conflict. By involving all stakeholders in the mediation process, including victims, perpetrators, and civil society actors, mediation can help to promote reconciliation and foster sustainable peace, which is especially helpful immediately after conflict and violence to build a stable civil-political system.

It is acknowledged that there remain many shortcomings of mediation, especially the use of mediation to resolve human rights violations. Power imbalances between parties may become even more evident, with the confidentiality of the process exacerbating alternative ways of expression or public advocacy. The traditional principle of voluntariness in mediation also directly conflicts with what human rights advocates consider to be ideal with respect to resolving human rights violations. Voluntary mediation seems backwards because perpetrators should be brought to justice whether or not they voluntarily participate in resolving the abuse.[1] In contexts where negotiation is not native and is viewed as an imported concept, supported by the fabrication of informed consent activated by a third party, parties enter into mediation involuntarily.[2]

B. *The mediator in addressing human rights violations*

(1) *Ways of facilitating the mediation process to overcome challenges in addressing human rights violations*

Despite the above-mentioned shortcomings, it is argued that mediation remains valuable in resolving and moving on from human rights violations because the mediator can play a role in addressing some of these challenges. Informal justice has been deemed to exacerbate societal inequalities and entrenched power structures, but mediators who have been trained in customary, domestic, and international law and norms would be able to use this knowledge during mediations to ensure that both parties know and understand their rights.[1] Awareness and knowledge of power imbalances already place mediators in a position to correct this in the mediation process through creative solutions.

One such example is equalising access to mediation advocates. In one instance of a mediation in Sierra Leone between community members and a company accused of illegal land grabs, the company wanted to bring a lawyer to the mediations, but the mediator would only allow this if the company paid for the community members' lawyers as well.[1] If mediation is being considered as an option for conflict resolution, victims must be informed of all their rights and options before mediations begin so they can determine if it is a proper dispute resolution mechanism for their case. However, if a human rights abuse is grave enough, it must be resolved through formal legal channels.[3]

(2) *Appropriate mediators to mediate human rights violations*

Who are the mediators mediating human rights violations? Appropriate mediators would usually have to be seen to be impartial and unbiased, but the persons or organisations taking the mediatory role would depend on the parties involved.

Where both parties are states, a neutral international body or regional treaty-based mechanism would be most suitable. For example, in the Pakistan–India water conflict over the Indus Basin region, the right of access to water was infringed upon. Pakistan approached the international community and the World Bank took the initiative of mediating between India and Pakistan for the allocation and distribution of river water between the two countries. As a result of the mediation of the World Bank, the Indus Waters Treaty was signed by the leaders of both countries, Indian Prime Minister Jawaharlal Nehru and Pakistani Field Marshal Ayub Khan, in 1960.[4]

Between private actors, a non-governmental organisation (NGO) or state-funded mediation programme can step in, especially in rural areas where accessibility to formal judicial systems may present an issue. In 1998, Malawi instituted a mediation programme for confronting human rights abuses, providing for mediation while ensuring that parties are not intimidated into settling a dispute.[1] Occasionally, states may step in to mediate another country's internal conflict, such as the unusual case of China playing lead mediator in peace talks between warring factions in South Sudan, driven by its own commercial interests as South Sudan had been providing five percent of China's oil imports.[5] However, a state's mediation of the internal affairs of another state is not recommended as it is often frowned upon by the international community, characterised as foreign interference, and studies have found that it may decrease the likelihood of settlement.[6]

Where it is state actors that have violated the rights of a community and are seeking to move forward, the establishment of national human rights institutions (NHRIs) is also possible. Even though NHRIs are funded by the state, they must be seen to be independent from the state in terms of having legal, operational, and financial autonomy to be accepted as impartial mediators. Compared to international or regional human rights bodies, they have the advantage of being closer to the ground and may be staffed by people who speak the native language, are conversant with local customs, and can best engage government officials to procure effective results. The twenty-five-member Indonesian Human Rights Commission, established by Presidential Decree No. 50 in June 1993, is one such example that has earned a substantial degree of public trust. For instance, 1406 out of 1927 cases handled by the Commission in 1996 were settled. This indicates that the common citizen recognises that the Commission is sufficiently independent from the government and sufficiently effective and worth appealing to without fear of repercussions.[7]

That being said, NHRIs have varying functions and degrees of effectiveness across countries. The Malaysian Human Rights Commission, SUHAKAM, plays a mediatory role not in organising formal mediation sessions but in acting as an intermediary between the state and the community in human rights complaints. It takes human rights complaints from aggrieved groups and produces annual reports and recommendations for Parliament. However, it has been viewed as ineffective and having only a "therapeutic role", allowing people to express their grievances in the hope that these would be heard, if not attended to, and providing a stabilising function by sustaining hope that a matter will find resolution within the legal order. Eventually, the fact that the government has ignored SUHAKAM prompted the criticism that it is "a warehouse for storing reports and memorandums", which the government will systematically ignore.[8] But in recent years, SUHAKAM has played a bigger role. For the first and only time in 2018, Parliament finally debated SUHAKAM's Annual Report, which SUHAKAM considered as signalling a commitment to improve human rights.[9] SUHAKAM has also shown that it is not afraid to confront the Malaysian government over certain human rights matters, for example in organising rallies urging the government to become party to the United Nations International Convention on the Elimination of All Forms of Racial Discrimination (ICERD). There have even been cases of enforced disappearances with respect to religious minorities in Malaysia brought before SUHAKAM, in which SUHAKAM commenced a public inquiry and a subsequent report as a platform for the aggrieved family to gain their right to a remedy allegedly caused by the state. SUHAKAM as an NHRI can thus be evaluated as allowing the public to gain access to some kind of remedy for alleged human rights violations, mediating complaints where the state is more willing to discuss options of moving forward, and acting as adjudicator where the state is unwilling to acknowledge wrongdoing.

C. *Effectiveness of mediation to address human rights violations*

(1) *Standard of effectiveness*

There is no uniform standard for evaluating the effectiveness of mediation — any result generated may potentially be praised or criticised by different standards. An agreed-upon outcome may be viewed as a good alternative to litigation by one party, but may then be critiqued for not going far enough to redress wrongs for another party. Time is also a factor, as the commitment of parties towards their agreement may only be assessed with time.

Despite the various standards towards measuring effectiveness, this chapter will consider two key criteria in evaluating the effectiveness of mediation in the context of human rights violations:

1. Addressing accountability for human rights violations through the mediation process and outcome; and
2. Involvement and reconciliation of parties through the mediation process and outcome.

(2) *Effectiveness and shortcomings of mediation in Asian case studies*

In the Philippines, the Transitional Justice and Reconciliation Commission (**"TJRC"**) was established as a part of the ongoing Bangsamoro peace process to provide an appropriate mechanism for transitional justice and reconciliation. This process follows the Moro conflict in the Mindanao region of the Philippines, which may be described as one of the most intractable conflicts in modern Philippines' history,[10] whereby an estimated 120,000 people have been killed[11] and countless others have suffered serious human rights violations. In circumstances marked by ongoing or protracted violent conflict, amnesties are often instituted as the means of ending an "urgent and grave situation" or halting or "avert[ing] mass violence".[12] However, by definition, they foreclose the possibility of future criminal (and sometimes civil) prosecutions.[13]

This leaves perpetrators free to continue "enacting violence with impunity",[14] particularly in contexts in which the continuation of conflict serves their personal and political interests.

The TRJC has a strong anti-impunity stance, yet leaves room for amnesties to be granted, accepting that in certain circumstances, amnesties may remain a legitimate strategy to entice warring parties to sign peace agreements and encourage them to abide by their terms. Further, the TRJC primarily mediates between warring factions rather than between the victims and perpetrators of human rights violations. Consequently, there is little room for accountability of human rights violations, and insufficient involvement of and consultation with victims and civil society.[15] However, there are other victims who have received reparation and recognition as victims of human rights violations during the Marcos regime. In 2018, about 11,100 victims of human rights violations who suffered under Marcos finally received monetary compensation.[16] This shows a partial monetary remedy solution that is not inclusive of all victims.

In Thailand's far south, the root cause of conflict has been the competitive power struggle between the Malay Muslim movement and the Thai state, known as the South Thailand Insurgency. The violence from the clash between militant insurgents and Thai security agencies, deriving from long-time tensions, heightened in late 2001 and further escalated beginning in January 2004. From January 2004 to October 2017, there were 19,548 violent incidents, 6,669 deaths, and 13,211 people injured from violence and counter-violence.[17]

In 2005, the National Reconciliation Commission (NRC) was created. This independent commission sought to resolve South Thailand Insurgency problems by providing a public space for dialogue and meeting among government officials, religious leaders, and local leaders to find a solution in the region. The state also adjudged a multitude of human rights violation cases by utilising a policy of "healing" for victims in the deep south of Thailand, through monetary compensation and the provision of scholarships and funds for careers. However, these lacked the effectiveness and equality of the judicial process (retributive justice) for victims and families involving both Malay Muslims and

Buddhists.[18] Women's organisations, such as Civic Women for Peace (Civic Women) and the Peace Agenda of Women (PAOW), children's organisations, such as the Nusantara Foundation For Human Rights and Development (Nusantara), and other development foundations have all stepped in to devise remedies to improve the situation of local people. Besides monetary compensation for victims and societal healing, another kind of reparation is apologising to families who have suffered from the violence. This has come in the form of apologies from state leaders in the Takbai district and in the Toh Chud cases.[19]

However, because many of the separatist groups are decentralised and lack clear leadership, it is difficult to negotiate or mediate with them as a cohesive entity. This also means that guarantees of non-recurrence of human rights violations can be difficult to procure, and existing programmes and mediations have not assured safety for victims and their families during the ongoing conflict.[18]

(3) *Recommendations*

Following from the above-mentioned principles and case studies, some recommendations can be made regarding the use of mediation to address human rights violations in an Asian context.

First, the leaders of all stakeholder groups need to be included in the mediation and peace processes, including perpetrators and victims alike. In particular, a major obstacle has been the refusal of the Thai state to provide amnesty to insurgent leaders. Despite criticism about amnesty, such legal reassurances may be needed to attract the participation of insurgent leaders in open talks and mediations.[20] International experience shows that even if initial grievances are addressed, violence will not decrease unless those who control the means of violence on both sides enter into mediation to work towards peace.

Secondly, partnerships with civil society, such as government and community-based actors like NHRIs and NGOs, can provide a legitimising function towards the acceptance of a non-legal alternative dispute resolution method such as mediation, as such actors can help to educate victims on their rights, correct cases of power imbalance, and provide additional resources for remedies.

III. Conclusion

Mediation is a viable solution to addressing human rights violations in Asian societies. It is reconciliatory, helping to rebuild trust between state actors and civil society in tenuous civil-political contexts, and avoids recourse to overburdened court systems. Many disadvantages of mediation can be intentionally mitigated through creative solutions in facilitating the mediation process, such as by involving civil society actors to correct power imbalances, educating victims on their rights, or even allowing victims to act as the mediators themselves.

That being said, where mediation has been used to address human rights in Asian societies, it has had limited effectiveness, especially in engaging all stakeholders, including the perpetrators and the victims of human rights abuses. It is recommended that while mediation remains voluntary, all stakeholder groups should be included and involved in the mediation process so as to represent the agency and interests of the groups. Despite criticisms of granting amnesty, it may be necessary to draw parties to discussions and mediations to move forward in the peace process. While monetary compensation is better than nothing, future mediations could explore other options that might meet more interests of parties, for example by issuing formal acknowledgement and apologies for harm and abuse caused during conflicts.

Ultimately, mediation is possible and valuable to bring parties forward even after violent conflict and human rights violations. States and civil society actors can improve upon the use of mediation in transitional justice and peace processes to overcome challenges and contextualise them to Asia in ways that aim to engage all stakeholders, that are satisfactory to parties, and that are sustainable in the long run.

https://doi.org/10.1142/9789819801268_0002

Chapter 2

The Choice of Law issue in Article 5(1)(a) of the Singapore Convention

Teo Sheng Wei Jeriel

I. Introduction

The Singapore Convention on Mediation[1] (**"SCM"**) is a multilateral treaty developed by the United Nations Commission on International Trade Law (**"UNCITRAL"**). The general object and purpose of the SCM is to create a harmonised process for the recognition and enforcement of international mediated settlement agreements,[2] loosely based on the process of recognition and enforcement of foreign arbitral awards under the New York Convention (**"NYC"**).[3]

Under Art 3 SCM, a Party to the Convention "shall" recognise and enforce a settlement agreement according to its own rules of procedure, and subject to any other requirements in the treaty.[4]

This obligation of recognition and enforcement is subject to, *inter alia,* Art 5 SCM, which sets out the substantive grounds for refusing relief under the treaty. Art 5(1)(a) SCM states the following[5]:

> "The competent authority of the Party to the Convention where relief is sought under article 4 may refuse to grant relief at the request of the party against whom the relief is sought only if that party furnishes to the competent authority proof that…[a] party to the settlement agreement was under some incapacity".

In this chapter, the appropriate choice of law rule to be applied in adjudicating issues of capacity under Art 5(1)(a) SCM is addressed, from the perspective of a Singapore court asked to grant relief under Art 3 SCM. Three possible approaches are set out: The first approach is to leave it to the private international law of the forum (the "private international law approach"). The second approach is to eschew choosing any particular law and, instead, adopt an autonomous definition of the phrase "some incapacity" (the "autonomous interpretation approach"). The third approach is to apply a "validation principle", that is, to apply any law that is potentially applicable to the settlement agreement that will cause the settlement agreement to be valid (the "validation principle approach").

In this chapter, it is argued that the private international law approach should be adopted. Art 5(1)(a) SCM does not contain an express choice of law rule. The inference to be drawn from this deliberate exclusion is that the drafters intended for the relevant choice of law rule to be supplied by the private international law of the forum.

In this chapter, the application of the autonomous interpretation approach, as well as the validation principle approach, is rejected. The autonomous interpretation approach is rejected because the SCM itself supplies too little material to support such an interpretive approach.

The validation principle approach is rejected because it fundamentally misunderstands the purpose of the incapacity doctrine and undercuts its protective rationale. It presumes that the parties would have intended for their settlement agreement to be valid, but it misses the point that intention is not germane to the analysis of capacity.

This chapter proceeds as follows. Section II will set out in detail the reason why the determination of the law on capacity should be left to the private international law of the forum. Section III analyses the "validation principle" and the "autonomous interpretation" approaches, and explains why they should be rejected. Section IV concludes the chapter.

II. The Private International Law Approach

Under the private international law approach, the choice of law issue is resolved by reference to the private international law of the forum.[6] This approach takes as its starting point the proposition that Art 5(1)(a) SCM does not expressly or impliedly set out any choice of law rule. In the absence of an express choice of law rule, the relevant national court may look to its own private international law to supply the relevant rule.

By way of illustration, it is submitted that Singapore is likely then to apply either the law of the country with which the contract is most closely connected or the law of the contracting parties' domicile and residence, whichever validates the contract.[7]

To be clear, although it is submitted that Singapore is likely to adopt a validation principle, this is only insofar as the validation principle is an emanation of its own private international law. Another state with a differing approach to private international law may therefore apply a different rule.

A plain reading, as well as the legislative history of the provision, demonstrates that the drafters deliberately excluded a choice of law rule from Art 5(1)(a) SCM.

Firstly, unlike other provisions in Art 5 SCM, the text of Art 5(1)(a) SCM itself does not expressly set out a choice of law rule. In contrast, Art 5(1)(b)(i) SCM provides the following[8]:

> "The settlement agreement sought to be relied on is null and void, or incapable of being performed, **under the law to which the parties have validly subjected it** or failing any indication thereon, under the law deemed applicable by the competent authority of the Party to the Convention where relief is sought under article 4". (emphasis added)

Art 5(1)(b)(i) is *in pari materia* with the provisions dealing with the nullity of an arbitration agreement under Art V(1)(a) NYC. The phrase "under the law to which the parties have validly subjected it" has been interpreted as a choice of law rule incorporating the governing law of the arbitration agreement.[9] The inference to be drawn from this comparison is that the drafters deliberately omitted a choice of law rule from Art 5(1)(a) SCM.

Secondly, a review of the *travaux preparatoires* demonstrates that the drafters of the SCM deliberately excluded a choice of law rule from the Art 5(1)(a) SCM because the inclusion of a choice of law rule in the context of the NYC proved to be problematic. Like the SCM, the NYC also provides, in Art V(1)(a), that incapacity is a ground for refusing recognition and enforcement. The relevant part of Art V(1)(a) NYC (the "incapacity ground") reads as follows:

> "Recognition and enforcement of the award may be refused, at the request of the party against whom it is invoked, only if that party furnishes to the competent authority where the recognition and enforcement is sought, proof that: The parties to [the arbitration agreement] were, **under the law applicable to them**, under some incapacity..." (emphasis added)

This provides a choice of law rule in the form of the phrase "under the law applicable to them" (the "personal law rule"). This chapter refers to this phrase as the personal law rule, because of the following[10]:

> "This provision makes clear that capacity is to be determined not by the law chosen by the parties, but rather by 'the law applicable to them' or their 'personal law', which for natural persons refers to the law of their nationality or domicile".

This rule has, however, been criticised for its circularity. Commentators have referred to it as a "half-way",[11] or "pseudo",[12] choice of law rule. The phrase "under the law applicable to them" has no substantive content of its own. As noted by Lord Hamblen and Lord Leggatt,[13] "[c]learly, referring simply to 'the law applicable to [the parties]' does not by itself determine which law is applicable to them". The phrase was therefore otiose. Despite purporting to create a choice of law rule, in interpreting the incapacity ground under Art V(1)(a) NYC, the forum would still have to apply its own private international law to determine the "law applicable".[14]

The drafters of the SCM were aware of these criticisms and deliberately excluded the personal law rule for that reason. As noted in the Report of Working Group II, Art 5(1)(a) SCM was modelled closely after the incapacity ground in Art V(1)(a) NYC. The personal law rule was excluded, because "[the personal law rule] ... was viewed as providing an incomplete and potentially misleading conflict-of-laws rule".[15]

Having established that Art 5(1)(a) SCM does not set out a choice of law rule, it is submitted that the forum state should apply its own private international law to determine the correct choice of law. This approach is in line with the academic consensus surrounding the incapacity ground in Art V(1)(a) NYC. As noted by one leading commentator,[16]

> "The applicable law in such a case is determined by the conflict of law rules of the forum in which recognition or enforcement of the award (or recognition of the arbitration agreement is sought".

It is submitted that this is in line with the SCM drafters' intentions. In one of the working papers discussing the ideal approaches to drafting the SCM, the drafters noted that "the instrument should not address the laws applicable with respect to defences in the enforcement procedure, with the assumption that the enforcing authority or the court seized with the matter would usually apply the conflict-of-law rules at the place of enforcement and where relevant, consideration of the parties' choice of law in the settlement agreement".[17]

Further to this, the justification for adopting a private international law approach in the context of Art 5(1)(a) SCM is stronger than in Art V(1)(a) NYC. As observed by Born,[18]

> "Some commentators have suggested that Article V(1)(a) does not resolve the question of the law applicable to issues of capacity, leaving it to national courts in individual Contracting States to apply their own choice-of-law rules".

Arguably, the observation that "Article V(1)(a) does not resolve the question of the law applicable to issues of capacity" applies *a fortiori* in the context of Art 5(1)(a) SCM, which does not have *any* choice of law rule at all.

III. The Alternative Approaches

A. *The autonomous approach*

One alternative approach to the choice of law conundrum raised by Art 5(1)(a) SCM is to take an "autonomous" interpretation of the term "some kind of incapacity". Such an approach was proposed by Ragno.[19] In this view, it is not self-evident that, in the absence of a choice of law rule, a private international law approach should apply. Instead, the absence of a choice of law rule might be indicative that an autonomous definition of capacity should apply instead.

In his view, a court called upon to interpret the phrase "some kind of incapacity" should avoid applying "domestic lenses", whether by usage of the substantive law of the forum or by *renvoi* to the substantive law of another country.[20] Instead, the competent authority of the forum should develop a definition that is unique to the NYC.[21]

The justification for an autonomous approach is that a purely private international law approach would have the effect of fragmenting the definition of "capacity". In his view,[22]

> "The only way to promote uniformity in the application of the New York Convention and to avoid a situation leading 'to unilateral interpretation and divergences between the rights and obligations of both the Contracting states and individuals' is by pursuing an autonomous interpretation of the notion of incapacity and of the corresponding notion of capacity".

He proposes the following interpretive methodology. A textual analysis of the phrase "the parties were…under some incapacity", as it appears in Art V(1)(a) NYC, suggests that capacity is a subjective condition of a party to the arbitration agreement. Therefore, capacity can only refer to some attribute or quality that is personal or inherent to the party to the arbitration agreement.[23]

Applying this logic, capacity can only include general capacity, which he defines as "the capacity to have rights and duties",[24] and contractual capacity, which is the capacity of natural persons or legal entities to enter into contracts.[25] However, it does not include subjective arbitrability, or arbitrability *ratione personae.*[26] Subjective arbitrability refers to the restrictions imposed by a legal person, usually a state, on its own capacity to enter into contracts.[27]

Having established that capacity only refers to general and contractual capacity, and not subjective arbitrability, Ragno proposes that general and contractual capacity should be determined with reference to the "law applicable [to the parties]", as the wording of the Art V(1)(a) NYC demands.

There are two observations to be made about Ragno's proposed interpretation. The first is that he is prepared to accept that the private international law approach should apply in determining questions of general or contractual capacity.[28] Ragno's proposed interpretation merely addresses the question of whether to characterise subjective arbitrability as an issue of capacity. He declines to take a purely autonomous approach to incapacity, and rightly so. As noted by Alexander, Chong, and Giordgadze,[29]

> "[E]lucidating the concept of 'incapacity' from an autonomous perspective could be all but a search in vain, as one has to account for the various idiosyncratic national rules on determining capacity across several jurisdictions, which point in various (sometimes opposing) directions The difficulty encountered is a result of the fact that there are fundamental differences to determine capacity under various governing laws".

The second observation is that Ragno's proposed interpretation is ultimately superficial. The SCM itself does not supply sufficient material to inform a purely self-referential definition of incapacity. Indeed, as noted in the *travaux preparatoires,* incapacity was recognised as a defence against recognition and enforcement precisely because it "was commonly found in international instruments as well as domestic legislation".[30] It is highly unlikely that the drafters would have intended for it to have a definition entirely unique to the SCM.

Ragno himself seems to recognise the futility of this endeavour and does not commit to a fully autonomous definition of incapacity. However, because he does not commit to such a project, his "definition", if it can be called that at all, is superficial. It merely restates the dictionary definition with the added gloss that the purported incapacity must relate to a subjective quality of the party alleging incapacity.

Ragno's autonomous interpretation is thus a solution in search of a problem. His definition is only useful insofar as it resolves the question of whether to characterise subjective arbitrability as a question of capacity. However, it is unclear why that conundrum could not be resolved by reference to domestic law.[31]

B. *The validation principle approach*

The validation principle approach proceeds from an entirely different starting point. The validation principle proceeds on the basis that Art 5(1)(a) SCM does in fact provide a choice of law rule, as argued by Alexander, Chong, and Giordgadze. In particular, they argue that the deliberate omission of the personal law rule is that it "advocates for a more expansive choice of law concept to be applied when the issue of incapacity is raised as a defence".[32]

However, it is not at all clear why this should be the case; the more natural explanation for the drafters' deliberate omission of a choice of law rule is that they did not wish to supply a choice of law rule. As explained earlier, the drafters' intention in omitting a choice of law rule was to avoid the problems caused by the personal law rule.

Nonetheless, proceeding *arguendo* that Art 5(1)(a) SCM does in fact supply a choice of law rule, Alexander, Chong, and Giordgadze conceive of the validation principle in the following terms:[33]

> "The 'validation principle' … posits that parties, by virtue of their participation in international commerce, must be taken to have desired for their contractual arrangements with respect to all matters of their transaction (including the effects flowing from a choice of governing law) to be validly concluded, enforceable and performed to their best effect".

To place such a premium on the presumed intentions of the parties to the settlement agreement is however to misconstrue the role that intention plays in contract law. This can be illustrated with specific reference to mental capacity. When a party lacks mental capacity, the inference is not that the party did not intend to enter into that settlement agreement. Rather, the inference is that the intention to be bound was procured in an unfair manner, such that it would be inequitable for the court to allow the capable party to rely on or enforce that contract.[34] Furthermore, mental incapacity only renders a contract voidable and not void *ab initio*.[35] If a party lacked an intention to create legal relations, then no contract would come into existence in the first place.[36]

In conclusion, the validation principle sidesteps the rationale for the incapacity defence. It is not enough to demonstrate that the parties intended to be bound; the question that the court must satisfy itself on is whether that intention was procured in an unfair manner. This in turn raises the question of whose substantive standards of fairness are to be employed. Resorting to the standard that validates the contract is therefore a purely circular solution.

IV. Conclusion

In closing the discussion on Art 5(1)(a) SCM, it should be observed that Art 5(1)(a) SCM should never have been included in the SCM at all. The drafting approach towards Art 5 SCM appears to have been to amalgamate language contained in Art II NYC with Art V NYC.[37] This has resulted in Art 5 becoming internally incoherent.

Typically, capacity is treated as a vitiating factor in contract, akin to other doctrines such as fraud, duress, or mistake. In an initial proposal, Art 5(1)(a) SCM would have contained the various grounds for vitiating a contract such as coercion or fraud.[38] However, the references to coercion and fraud were removed, because the drafters felt that vitiating factors were already encapsulated in Art 5(1)(b) SCM, which tracks Art II(3) NYC. The result of this is that Art 5(1)(a) SCM is left being otiose.

Worse still, Art 5(1)(b) SCM supplies a choice of law rule, whereas Art 5(1)(a) SCM does not. Despite being similar to other vitiating factors, capacity is being treated as *sui generis*, as far as the choice of law analysis goes. Where all other vitiating factors are subject to the law governing the settlement agreement, capacity is subject to the vagaries of the forum's private international law. Yet, it is impossible to escape this conundrum because of the clear distinctions in the language between Arts 5(1)(a) and 5(1)(b) SCM.

https://doi.org/10.1142/9789819801268_0003

Chapter 3

At the Intersection of Justice: Where Victim–Offender Mediations and Singapore's Criminal Justice System Meet

Chan Wayde

I. Introduction

There has been an encouraging movement in advocacy for Victim–Offender Mediation (**"VOM"**) worldwide, as shown by a recent increase in academic literature on the matter. This chapter stands firmly in support of introducing VOM in Singapore for all offences with identifiable victims and seeks to refine and respond to suggestions raised in both local and foreign literature. Section II of this chapter discusses the present state of Criminal Mediation in Singapore, while Section III posits that VOM should be offered after an offender has been charged but before sentencing. Section IV then elaborates specifically on how VOM applies to sentencing law. Finally, Section V addresses some procedural safeguards of VOM, before concluding with Section VI.

II. VOM and Criminal Mediation — The Singapore Approach

Criminal Mediation in Singapore is a judge-led process where the victim and the offender meet to discuss the offence at hand with the goal of reaching a resolution for the matter to be dispensed with. Criminal Mediation is indeed a form of VOM. Presently, Criminal Mediation in Singapore is limited to two narrow and specific scenarios[1]:

1. First, where the victim files a police report and the police decide not to pursue the matter. After this, the victim files a Magistrate's

Complaint and the Magistrate finds that there is sufficient merit to proceed on the Complaint and thereafter refers the matter to Criminal Mediation.

2. Second, where the victim files a police report, and after investigation, the police find that an offence has indeed been disclosed, but the police decline to take further action against the offender. The victim then pursues a Magistrate's Complaint, after which the Magistrate refers the matter to Criminal Mediation.

Furthermore, Magistrate's Complaints are limited only to offences punishable by imprisonment of 3 years or less.[2]

Criminal Mediation is not an option in the following circumstances[3]:

1. The Attorney-General Chambers (**"AGC"**) decide to take over the case and formally prosecute the offender;
2. The AGC and/or the police, upon investigation, give the offender a conditional or unconditional stern warning;
3. The AGC and/or the police decide that no offence has been disclosed; or
4. The Magistrate's Complaint is withdrawn.

It is unsurprising that Criminal Mediation only occurs under limited circumstances, considering the AGC's and police's extensive control over each file.[4]

While the AGC's and police's active involvement in alleged offences is highly commendable and is a testament to Singapore's safety, their intervention often benefits the state, not the victim. This is because criminal cases in Singapore are mostly (barring rare private prosecutions) brought by the Public Prosecutor against the offender. The victim is often relegated to the role of a "complaining witness"[5] and plays a limited role in the conduct of the prosecution and the manner in which the offender is punished.[6]

If the court finds the offender guilty, in that the victim's complaints are admitted to (where the offender pleads guilty) or proven beyond reasonable doubt (where the offender claims trial) the offender is typically sentenced to imprisonment, a fine, or other corrective measures. These punishments, however, do not directly remedy the harm caused to the victim, and any fines and financial penalties imposed are payable to the state, not the victim.[7] These victims may not have the financial resources to pursue civil claims and might be left without relief without intervention from the criminal courts.[8,9]

While Singapore law allows criminal courts to impose compensation orders against the offender, compensation orders have been held to be limited, owing to the difference in causation, apportioning liability, and procedure in criminal and civil cases.[10] Additionally, compensation orders do not consider the damage caused by dropped charges. Furthermore, the financial nature of compensation orders eschews the non-pecuniary aspects of the victim's recovery.[11]

Hence, it is submitted that an additional measure of VOM ought to be introduced in Singapore. While the author supports a previous work[12] to introduce VOM for sexual offences, the author suggests expanding VOM to all offences with identifiable victims.[13] Not all offences will see a need for VOM,[14] but it is hoped that VOM can be progressively introduced to all relevant offences.

III. VOM and Prosecutions — A Legal Collaboration

There have been diverse views over when VOM is most appropriate to be conducted. There are generally three entry points in a criminal case's life cycle for VOM to enter the picture[15]:

1. Pre-Charging Stage;
2. Pre-Sentencing Stage; and
3. Post-Sentencing Stage.

While there has been support for VOM to be introduced at each stage,[16,17] the author posits that VOM should only be introduced at the Pre-Sentencing and Post-Sentencing Stages. This chapter focuses on the Pre-Sentencing Stage.

A. *The proposed approach*

It is submitted that the most appropriate approach is to conduct VOM during the period after the offender has been formally charged in court, but before he/she is sentenced post-conviction. This applies regardless of whether the offender pleads guilty to the charge or claims a trial. This means that while VOM can commence any time after the suspect has been charged, it must conclude before the judge imposes a sentence.

Beyond the psychological and financial benefits of VOM to both the victim and the offender, VOM should also play a part in the offender's criminal proceedings. Upon completion of VOM, the AGC ought to first review whether there still remains a public interest to continue the prosecution of the offender in light of the completed VOM. Answering in the negative would mean that, under the AGC's prosecutorial guidelines, the prosecution must be discontinued.[18]

In the event that the AGC is still of the opinion that there is a reasonable prospect of conviction, but there is no longer a public interest to prosecute the offender post-VOM, the AGC should then apply to the court for a discharge amounting to an acquittal (**"DATA"**)[19] and impose a stern warning. A stern warning is a non-binding opinion that an offence has been committed, but no prosecution will be made.[20] The effect of a stern warning is an acquittal.

For clarity, the author humbly submits that the above-mentioned approach is only likely to happen in a minority of cases. VOM serves to protect both the victim's and the offender's interests. However, the AGC is the guardian of *public* interest. Prosecuting in the public interest has been defined as prosecutions *"in the name of the public"*, *"for the good of the public"*, *"according to values expected by the public"*, and *"in the eye of the public"*.[21] Furthermore, *"criminal prosecutions are brought not to further the private interests of the victim, but to further the larger public interest"*.[22] Thus, the AGC may carry on with prosecutions even if victims have been compensated and choose to drop their complaints.[23] This is because offenders answer "*not to the victim alone, but to the public in general*".[24,25]

The more likely scenario is for the court, when deciding the offender's sentence post-conviction, to take into consideration the level of remorse and restitution the offender has showed during VOM. This will be elaborated further in Section IV.

B. *Benefits of the proposed approach and responses to criticism*

The proposed approach is best observed for a wide timeline in which VOM can be introduced. This recognises that victims and offenders alike may not be willing to undergo VOM at the first instance, nor is it always appropriate for victims and offenders to undergo VOM immediately.[26] Thus, given that some time will have elapsed before the offender is charged, victims and offenders are likely to be in better emotional states to undergo VOM, thereby enhancing the potential efficacy of VOM.

Furthermore, the structure of the proposed approach does not require the criminal proceedings to halt while awaiting VOM in most instances. VOMs can occur alongside pre-trial and trial proceedings as their respective procedures do not interfere with one another. The AGC may apply for a DATA anytime, and the sentencing decision just needs to post-date the conclusion of VOM. Of course, it is open to the courts to stay proceedings for VOM (and vice versa) in complex circumstances. This shows the high level of flexibility that the proposed approach brings, saving all parties time and resources.

Admittedly, there are some rightful concerns with allowing an offender to claim trial and request for VOM at the same time since VOM is predicated on the offender being willing to acknowledge and own up to his/her wrongdoings.[27,28] In response, offenders claim trial for many reasons,[29] and not necessarily out of a lack of remorse. For example, the offender could admit to having caused hurt to the victim but may claim trial to contend whether such hurt was caused voluntarily or negligently. Justice for the victim and closure for the offender should not be at odds with the offender's right to a fair trial,[30] and should instead coexist.

Furthermore, if an offender claims trial and engages in victim-blaming or challenging his/her involvement in the offence, the judge may decide that the offender's request or consent to enter VOM was merely premised on an attempt to seek a lower sentence, rather than genuine remorse.

C. *Why VOM should not be offered at the Pre-Charging Stage*

While there are certain benefits for stretching VOM beyond the Pre-Sentencing Stage to include the Pre-Charging Stage, such as the possibility of disposing off offences which do not meet the public interest threshold for prosecution post-VOM, the technical operations of the criminal justice system and mediation militate against such a proposal.

Firstly, as mentioned earlier, VOM alone is unlikely to lower an offender's prosecution below the public interest threshold. While doing so will reduce the caseload that passes through the criminal courts, in practice it is, and ought to be, unlikely to occur.

Secondly, VOMs should be court-based mediations, rather than private mediations. This is because, as will be further illustrated in Part V, the level of confidentiality and procedure in VOMs may be substantially different from generally held perceptions of mediation. Private mediators may be faced with dilemmas between their ethical-confidentiality obligations and their disclosure obligations under the Mediation Act 2017[31] for criminal offences. It is preferable to institutionalise the VOM framework in the courts themselves, for instance, by amending the Rules of Court 2021.[32]

Furthermore, since a criminal offence is a wrongdoing against the public interest,[33] dealing with criminal offences ought to be brought into the public system, which includes the courts. Court-based mediation is already seen in Criminal Mediation, the Family Justice Courts, and various court clusters within the State Courts. Hence, extending court-based mediations to VOMs is most appropriate, and in order to bring any case with the potential for VOM into the public system, the AGC must first charge the offender in court.

D. *Further comments*

The author acknowledges that the introduction of VOMs does not patch all shortcomings. If the police investigation discloses an offence which is not further pursued, the victim can lodge a Magistrate's Complaint. However, if the AGC gives a stern warning, the Magistrate's Complaint closes without an avenue of recourse besides a civil claim. To this, the author proposes legal reform. If investigations disclose an offence but the

AGC gives a stern warning,[34] it should be open to the victim to pursue the matter privately via the Magistrate's Complaint, which may lead to Criminal Mediation or private prosecution.

IV. VOM and Sentencing — A Delicate Tango

The author submits that the VOM should be taken into account when deciding on the offender's sentence, which is the approach taken in the Netherlands,[35] but not to the extent of a full acquittal, which is the approach taken in the US.[36]

This part first discusses why VOM should not result in a full acquittal, before responding to criticisms about VOM having an effect on sentencing.

A. *VOM and the four sentencing principles*

In Singapore, there are four sentencing principles employed by the courts — Deterrence, Rehabilitation, Prevention, and Retribution/ Proportionate Punishment.[37] In particular, deterrence can be split into specific deterrence, which seeks to deter the offender from re-offending, or general deterrence, which serves to deter the public from committing similar offences.

VOM seeks to rehabilitate the offender by getting him or her to recognise his or her wrongdoings and move forward by seeking resolution and peace with the victim. VOM allows the offender to be heard, regardless of whether he/she is forgiven. In fact, in a US survey, more offender-respondents highlighted that they entered VOM to "speak their minds" rather than to mend relationships.[38]

Furthermore, VOM promotes specific deterrence. By reflecting on how the victim has suffered from the offence, coupled with the sense of humility and financial loss stemming from a settlement, the offender is less likely to re-offend.

However, VOM does not address three principles — General Deterrence, Prevention if the offender is a threat to public safety, and Retribution/Proportionate Punishment for the offence. While VOM might provide some mitigation, these principles remain vital, especially for serious offences. Hence, the offender cannot walk free just because he/she participated in VOM. The US model is criticised precisely because acquitting the offender post-VOM effectively disregards these principles.[39]

B. *VOM as a mitigating factor in sentencing*

The idea that participation in VOM should be a mitigating factor is a heated source of debate.[40] On the one hand, participating in VOM shows remorse and gives the offender an avenue to provide some restitution to the victim. Furthermore, the victim may forgive the offender. On the other hand, participating in VOM may just be an afterthought to seek a lighter sentence. The author attempts to reconcile the opposing views on these mitigating factors.

1. *Forgiveness*

While forgiveness goes a long way in a victim's healing process, there is *"little place for forgiveness in the field of [Singapore]'s criminal law"*,[41] and forgiveness has been held not to be a mitigating factor except in exceptional circumstances.[42] Hence, arguing whether forgiveness stemming from VOM should be a mitigating factor is a non-starter.

2. *Remorse*

There have been criticisms that VOM only incentivises offenders to fake their remorse in hopes of a lighter sentence.[43] While the author acknowledges such a possibility, Singapore case law has held that the amount of mitigating weight given to a plea of guilt is relative to the extent the plea represents remorse.[44] Similarly, the courts are also in a good position to assess the remorse shown by the offender through VOM. Witnesses such as the mediator, any medical professional present, counsels, and the victims themselves may testify in court on the offender's behaviour during VOM. The courts may also screen through the process and outcome of VOM to assess the offender's remorse.

Furthermore, settlement agreements from VOM can be registered as court orders. Therefore, if the offender merely pretends to agree to a settlement during VOM but subsequently reneges on the agreement, he/she is liable for contempt of court.

Addressing how VOM and remorse ought to operate in practice in the courts, Singapore law has held that an earlier plea of guilt, provided it is a show of genuine remorse, ought to attract a higher sentencing discount as compared to pleading guilty during or after the trial.[45] The recent publication of the Sentencing Advisory Panel's *Guidelines on Reduction in Sentences for Guilty Pleas* further provides a structured framework which accords a greater discount in sentencing to offenders who plead guilty earlier. This recognizes that by pleading guilty, the offender has expressed remorse, spared the need for the victims and witnesses to testify, and saved public resources by avoiding a trial.[46]

One may be quick to conclude that if VOM is undertaken earlier, a greater sentencing discount ought to be applied. However, this may not always be the case. VOM requires genuine consent from both the offender and the victim.[47,48] Even if the offender wishes to enter VOM, the victim might not be ready and VOM is hence delayed, or even avoided. Therefore, the better approach is to make an assessment at the time when the offender requests for VOM and analyse whether such a request was made as a sign of genuine remorse or an attempt to get a lower sentence. While ultimately the offender's sentence will be affected by whether VOM has occurred, any lack of VOM ought to be assessed in the context of the willingness of both the victim and the offender to participate in VOM. Similarly, the mitigating effect of VOM must be viewed in the context of whether it is a sign of genuine remorse.

3. *Restitution*

Concerns have also been raised over whether restitution stemming from VOMs should be recognised as a mitigating factor.[49] In response, it must first be highlighted that restitution is a mitigating factor in Singapore.[50] However, the courts have also held that they are in a position to determine whether the restitution may be made out of genuine remorse or as an afterthought to secure a lower sentence.[51]

Unfortunately, the financial nature of restitution suggests that an offender with lesser means is less likely to benefit from restitution as a mitigating factor. This is not an issue which affects VOM alone but sentencing law in Singapore generally.

V. VOM and Processes — Reimagining Mediation

The author submits that traditional mediation principles should not bind VOM but instead adapt to best suit its purpose. The author will cover 2 points — the forward-looking nature of mediation and confidentiality.

A. *VOM and being forward-looking*

Facilitative mediation has always been classified as a forward-looking process.[52] Parties are encouraged not to attribute blame but to instead discuss forward-looking solutions.[53] This may not work for VOM, especially in the initial stages where both parties are trying to come to terms with the offence. Conversations about how the offence has affected the parties, allowing each to voice their respective sides of the story, are crucial in the parties' healing process. The goal need not be for parties to understand each other, but at least to be heard.

This will require more resources than traditional mediations. While mediations are often characterised by efficiency, typically reaching completion within hours or days, more sessions are needed to establish a constructive relationship between the VOM parties before moving into the forward-looking settlement process. This is why VOM processes in the Netherlands may last up to 6 weeks.[54] Furthermore, mediators should also have the relevant training to deal with emotionally charged situations to keep the sessions safe and constructive. It is recommended that co-mediation is adopted,[55] with a mental health specialist present to ensure the parties' emotional stability.[56] Before VOM commences, pre-VOM screening processes should be rigorously enforced to ensure the parties' suitability and motivations.[57]

B. *VOM and confidentiality*

In traditional mediation, confidentiality of the mediation process is key.[58] However, for VOM, the proceedings will need to be made known to external stakeholders who may not be present in the mediation room, such as the Prosecution, Defence Counsel, and the Judge. Furthermore, as suggested, those present at the mediation may be called to testify regarding the offender's remorse. Since Singapore has an open court system, confidentiality may be breached.[59,60] However, such concerns can be remedied with existing features of Singapore's court processes.

Safeguards exist to protect the confidentiality of legal proceedings. For example, the court may sit "in private",[61] sealing the courtroom off to everyone except approved persons.[62] This ensures any testimony given is confidential. Furthermore, Judges can direct for both parties' names to be redacted in the published Grounds of Decisions and order for sensitive evidence to be sealed.[63]

For example, parties must be informed of the stakeholders who will have access to the records of the mediation, the mediators' overriding duty to the court, and the safeguards in place to ensure any loss of confidentiality is kept to a minimum.

VI. Conclusion

VOM has the potential to expand the scope of Criminal Mediation in Singapore. It is hoped that through introducing VOM in Singapore, victims will be able to seek closure and be heard, offenders can make peace and work towards rehabilitation, and Singapore can benefit from reduced recidivism rates and effective resource management. VOM has seen a high success rate,[64] received high satisfaction ratings from its participants,[65] and is consistent with Singapore's alternative dispute resolution movement.[66]

With that said, VOM needs to be implemented in a way that does not compromise, but rather complements, established criminal law principles. This chapter has discussed several potential inconsistencies between VOM and criminal law. However, policymakers should not shy away from such conflicts by shunning VOM but instead work towards integrating VOM into the criminal law system to promote a safer Singapore.

https://doi.org/10.1142/9789819801268_0004

Chapter 4

Winning Together: Uncovering the Hidden Potential of Game Theory in Mediation

Chew Qing Xuan Kyna

I. Introduction

This chapter presents an interdisciplinary take on mediation by adopting the theoretical framework related to the field of economics and exploring the axioms of rationality and self-interest within mediation through the lens of game theory.

Game theory is the theoretical study of the tension between conflict and cooperation, applied through a mathematical model.[1] The model involves interdependent parties who are unaware of the full position of the counterparty within an interactive situation. Traditionally, the game theory model is based on the central assumption that the players are rational decision-makers set out to achieve the most optimal outcome.

(A) In this chapter, an overview of the game theory model will first be provided with an explanation of its applicability to mediation. **(B)** Next, a *prescriptive* approach to applying the game theory model to mediation is explored by adopting *Camerer's* three-step systemic approach. **(C)** Lastly, similar models that have been applied in mediation are identified and their utility in framing a mediator's perspective is highlighted.

A. *Game theory and its application in mediation*

(1) *Why game theory?*

Game theory is a novel interpretation of human behaviour that conceptualises and enables the analysis of interactions between agents within a strategic scenario to be conducted in a new mathematical language.[2] In this chapter, the strategic context contemplated is mediation.

This chapter opines that the application of game theory is both *suitable* and *beneficial* to mediation. On the former, the suitability of game theory is underlined by its internal consistency and mathematical foundations, which enables the theory to model strategic choices within dynamic interactive environments. On the latter, the tool forces the decision-maker to consider all variables present within a mediation setting; examples include the players' options, preferences, risk appetite, and reactions.[3]

As an amalgam of a variety of disciplines (such as, *inter alia,* law, psychology, and philosophy), mediation cannot take on the unyielding and rigid lens of the legal field. It is bound to benefit from an interdisciplinary take on the subject. This chapter submits that even the discipline of engaging in the construction of this mental model will enable mediators to take on a more nuanced view of the parties' respective positions. This may be coined as a "*prescriptive*" application of the game theory and will enable game theory to reframe disputes into a cooperative non-zero-sum relation (where the loss of one party does not translate to the loss of the other).

(2) *Dynamics of the game: mediation*

Before diving into the mechanics of the model, it is crucial to first identify the characteristics of mediation. In particular, its idiosyncrasies distinguish it from its peers — litigation and arbitration — and make it an especially suitable candidate for game theory.

Mediation is a unique dispute resolution mechanism that affords parties the autonomy and control to consider a variety of risks; this is lost in litigation — where a judge assumes control over procedural and substantive processes and decisions.

Within a mediation context, the mediator plays a vastly different role as compared to an arbitrator or a judge; this is because the mediator does not decide on the dispute on the basis of a "win–lose" outcome. That said, the mediator is similarly placed in an optimal position to facilitate the flow of information between parties. As will be elaborated on later in this chapter, these two factors are crucial to the application of the Game Theory model.

B. *Applying game theory to mediation*

One proposed model of applying game theory to mediation can be referenced from Colin F. Camerer's *Progress in Behavioral Game Theory*.[4] Camerer proposes the following three-step systemic approach incorporating both traditional and behavioural concepts in a coherent manner:

1. First, the traditional model of game theory is applied to represent the prevailing interests of parties within the game;
2. Second, the behavioural and/or situational factors that might affect these decisions are considered;
3. Third, these factors are integrated into the model.

Step one: Applying the Traditional Model of Game Theory

According to Durlauf and Blume,[5] the three ingredients within a bargaining game are as follows:

> *"(a) the status quo, or the disagreement point, that is, the arrangement that is expected to prevail if an agreement is not reached; (b) the presence of mutual gains from cooperation; and (c) the multiplicity of possible cooperative arrangements, which split the resulting surplus in different ways."*

In uncovering the definition of these three varying scenarios, economists such as Nash[6] proposed that a way to deal with the "disagreement point" is for players to introduce "threats", which act as a pressure point. It is therefore the job of the mediator to uncover this pinch point.

Envisioned within a mediation context, the "threat" is the cost of leaving this decision in the hands of the judiciary. This "threat" is powerful since it is a common point of certainty that underlies the position of both parties alike — that is, a common consensus that collaboration would mean an amicable settlement, whilst non-collaboration corresponds to the win–lose scenario in litigation.

In stark contrast to the "non-zero-sum" stance of mediation, litigation routinely presents a scenario that is worse than a "zero-sum" game or a "win–lose" situation. This change in position can often lead to mediation, allowing parties to gain a "positive sum" where both sides stand to benefit, while litigation lands parties in a "negative sum" where at least one party is bound to lose. As such, the potential cost of pursuing a "win" in litigation may not justify the resources and energy invested throughout the lifetime of a litigious process, especially where mediation presents the possibility of a more mutually beneficial outcome.

(1) *The Nash Equilibrium*

The Nash Equilibrium is a concept coined by mathematician John Nash, who explained that the best possible move of one player is bound to be a reaction to the best possible move of the counterparty.[7] As a corollary, parties need to account for the strategic considerations of the other within this interactive environment. This mathematical model reconceptualises the function of game theory from a *competitive* standpoint to a *cooperative* one since parties must engage in a *bargaining process* with each other.

In other words, it is assumed that each player in every game is aware of the equilibrium strategies of the other players. When parties meet at the point of equilibrium, none of the parties would draw a corresponding payoff or net benefit from a change in their strategies.

Applied to the mediation context, the Nash Equilibrium explains that within this medley of emotions comes a point of realisation for the mediating parties that a positive outcome is only possible through a successful settlement. As such, each player ought to behave in accordance with some bargaining strategy that aligns with their personal utility maximisation criterion. This dynamic would then lead to a point of equilibrium, which would illustrate probable cooperative solutions to the game.[8]

In principle, this means that mediators should be able to craft a model of the game in an extensive Bayesian form (a probability metric that is used to calculate the probability of an event happening) and determine the point of the equilibrium based on the set of data.[9] However, even though this *quantitative* approach is one possible way of applying game theory to mediation, this chapter envisions a more *prescriptive* approach — where the identification of the Nash Equilibrium within the context of the mediation helps mediators identify the potential point of compromise, also known as "*options*".

(2) *Focal point*

In reality, bargaining situations may lead us to different outcomes for settlement and, consequently, different equilibriums. This is reflected in the model developed by Thomas C. Schelling in 1960 which adapted John Nash's Nash Equilibrium to accommodate the *focal point concept*. The focal point reflects that the convergence is dependent on a multitude of factors, including the venue, time, and coordinating parties, thereby allowing for both *tacit* and *explicit* coordination between parties, within the confines of these varying scenarios and within parties' diverging interests.[10]

Within the context of mediation, the focal point can help facilitate and accelerate agreement. For instance, where both parties have identified a common interest in reducing costs, an incentive that aligns with this interest would be a crucial focal point.

(3) *The hidden cost of litigation*

One common pinch point that underlies all mediation is the cost of litigation. Parties often do not realise these hidden costs of litigation until the proceedings have ended and the losses have been incurred. Whilst parties may assume that the legal fees are the only costs borne, there are other hidden costs within litigation that might not appear as intuitively.[11] An understanding of these costs is crucial as mediators can apply pressure based on this common focal point.

(a) Decision costs
In litigation, judges are entangled within rigid rules of evidence. Evidence needs to be tested rigorously through complex discovery processes, production processes, and written pleadings. Significant time and costs are expended during these processes.

(b) Risk of loss costs
Within litigation, the court is bound to find in favour of one party over the other. In other words, there will always be a risk of loss. For the plaintiff, this means that there is a risk that their alleged losses will not be vindicated. Made even worse, the plaintiff may lose on grounds based on the defendant's counterclaim. Similarly, the defendant faces similar risks.

(c) Reputational cost
Court decisions are recorded and made public. For commercial parties, the risk of indelible public record and the consequent harm to its reputation cannot be understated. Confidential information may be published, allowing trade secrets or negative facts to be capitalised upon by competitors.

(d) Opportunity costs
When parties are entangled in long litigation processes, there are opportunity trade-offs in carrying out productive alternatives. For instance, for companies entangled in commercial disputes, the executives and managers are unable to use their productive hours and drive them towards profit-making activities, halting business activity. Further, there may also be relationship costs, where the healthy ongoing relationship between parties may inevitably be torn down by the adversarial nature of litigation. For certain matters, lost relationships may have sentimental or emotional implications, whilst for businesses, lost relationships directly translate to lost business opportunities.

(e) Gamesmanships costs
Litigation is littered with opportunities for lawyers to engage in strategic exploitation. Defensive strategies are commonly employed by parties in order to gain leverage or derail the litigation by making the litigation process oppressively difficult and expensive for the opposition. Whilst this is carried out for the sake of the parties, the costs fall similarly on their shoulders.

(f) Emotional and psychological costs
Parties engaged in long-drawn litigation experience emotional wear and tear. This typically applies throughout the litigation process but becomes especially pronounced when parties are called for vigorous cross-examination processes. Questioning tactics are often designed to corner witnesses into an implication of wrongdoing or deceit. This can traumatise individuals to different extents, but for most, the tantamount pressure of the process can severely damage one's psychological health.

Step two: Accounting for Behavioural and Situational Factors

In mediation, parties are bound to have different conceptions of an amicable solution, influenced by a myriad of *behavioural* and *situational* factors. Within a game theory model, this translates into multiple varying convergence points, further complicating the final solution to the game.[12]

Only a viable solution, accompanied by a worse payoff of non-settlement, will allow the parties to reach a settlement. A mediator's role is therefore to encourage cooperation by facilitating parties to come to a consensus on the focal point by sifting out details of their concerns.

The difficulty lies in balancing interests between parties of different backgrounds, ages, cultures, and biases.

(4) *Power disparity*

Power disparity can often distort the playing field. On this point, Chatterjee and Samuelson identified that the level of competitiveness can affect each parties' evaluation of the payoffs within a bargaining situation since it can alter the "best alternative to a negotiated agreement" (**"BATNA"**) of each player.[13] Typically, the alternative is the cost of litigation. Thus, the mediator's role here is to evaluate the BATNA values of each party and determine whether the cost of a judicial process is similar for both parties.

For instance, one party might have more relative experience dealing with similar litigation processes or the sum of lost cost may be more significant for one than the other. This asymmetry in position can make it difficult for a settlement to be reached. Another example could be within the context of a family dispute; in a situation where one party has no income whilst the other is the breadwinner for the family, the former might feel a heavier burden from litigation. The mediator's task will then transform into a balancing of the BATNA values between both parties.

Further, this may also be related to their risk appetite. When dealing with parties with different risk behaviours, varying decisions may be made based on the chance of identical gains or losses. In other words, when faced with the exact same potential gain, a rich man could much more easily place a bet as compared to a poor man because for a poor man, the possibility of the gain would not make up for the suffering caused by the possibility of loss.

(5) *Psychological bias*

Psychological biases are also another source of variance. As previously mentioned, the traditional game theory model was built on the assumption of rationality. However, with Camerer's approach, corrections are made by expanding on the assumption of rationality and factoring in possible "errors" and "preferences". These factors may then reflect a reordering of a party's priorities. Various values such as "justice" or "altruism", "commitment" or "ego" may also be incorporated.

A consideration of a party's psychological biases may also pull in Dutch social psychologist Hofstede's "*six cultural dimensions*"[14]: (1) *power distance*; (2) *individualism vs. collectivism*; (3) *masculinity vs. femininity*; (4) *uncertainty avoidance*; (5) *long-term vs. short-term orientation*; and (6) *indulgence vs. restraint.*

For instance, the first cultural dimension, "power distance" index (**"PDI"**), describes the level at which a culture accepts disparity in how authority is distributed amongst different figures. Countries like China might have a deference towards higher-"ranking" figures in a workplace setting or older members of society. Comparatively, a country like Denmark would rank low on the PDI. This psychological bias might make younger members of a mediation more susceptible to the opinions of an older member within a mediation involving parties from countries with a relatively higher PDI.

Another example would be in *individualistic* as compared to *collectivistic* cultures. A crucial part of the "option-finding" stage of the mediation involves selling a solution in a manner that is palatable. An individualistic culture would likely prioritise personal interests, whilst collectivistic cultures might be accepting of options that benefit the needs of the group as a whole. This allows mediators to package solutions better by emphasising personal or collective needs according to the parties' internal biases.

These psychological considerations are underlined by both neurophysiological foundations and linguistic foundations. The former prevents the player from being able to objectively process and gather information. The latter prevents players from being able to fully comprehend the true meaning of the information gathered, which would then impede decision-making.

Step 3: Integrating Behavioural and Psychological Factors

When integrating the factors contemplated under step two, it is worth noting the contextual factors that may further complicate a player's preferences. This observation was made by academics such as Tversky and Thaler, who pointed out the following[15]:

> *First, people do not possess a set of pre-defined preferences for every contingency. Rather, preferences are constructed in the process of making a choice or judgment. Second, the context and procedures involved in making choices or judgments influence the preferences that are implied by the elicited responses. In practical terms, this implies that behaviour is likely to vary across situations that economists consider identical.*

These deviations in preferences can be explained by the *framing effect,* which can be explained by a party's conceptions of the "*acts, outcomes, and contingencies associated with a particular choice*", and which is controlled, in part, by the way a problem has been formulated.[16] This is precisely where the mediator showcases their ability to reframe situations, at every point, in a manner that nudges the parties towards conciliation.

C. *The utility of modelling in mediation*

The use of prescriptive models to frame a mediator's perspective is not new to the mediation realm and its utility has been acknowledged in facilitating the mediator's role. One example of such a model is Riskin's Grid formulated by Professor Leonard Riskin, which bears an uncanny resemblance to a usual game theory model[17]:

Riskin's Grid has been widely recognised within the mediation community and has been used in training and evaluating mediators. Based on the Riskin model, there are two spectrums where mediators function — "facilitative" and "evaluative" — followed by a range of how "broadly" or "narrowly" the mediator could choose to define the issues within the mediation. The mediator can choose to function anywhere throughout the spectrum and may move along this range within one mediation at any given time.

MEDIATOR ORIENTATIONS
Role of Mediator

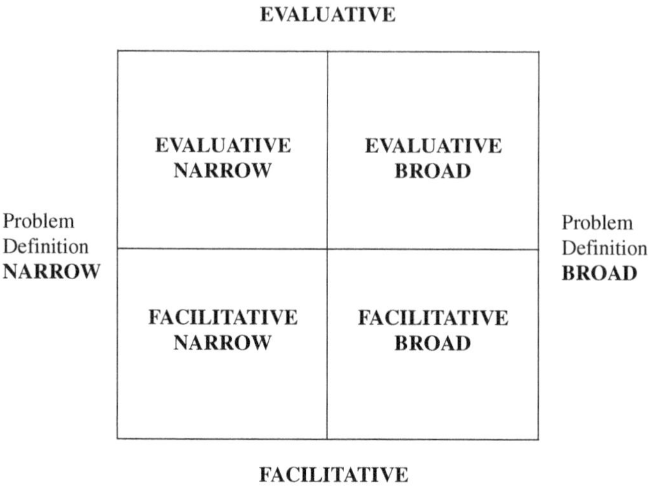

Source: Endnote 2.

The proposed solution in this chapter resembles the Riskin model in many ways. The game theory model similarly proposes that as the information structure within the mediation changes, with each new incoming piece of information, the game changes and a new solution may surface. The game theory model is therefore a suitable and beneficial tool to identify these changes in the game and model them in a manner that generates better payoffs for parties, and should not be shied away from for its unorthodox nature.

II. Conclusion

This chapter presents an interdisciplinary perspective on mediation, drawing on the insights of economic models to foster a more creative approach to resolving disputes within mediation.

The role of the mediator in this model is to identify the game by evaluating the attitude of clients, investigating emotions, recognising signals, and identifying interests. Most experienced mediators do this intuitively even without the assistance of the game theory model. However, the plotting of the model is a thought exercise that structures the mediator's perception of the game in a theoretical and concrete manner. Further, the flexibility of the model to account for behavioural, psychological, and contextual influences also allows it to accommodate the multiplicity of situations that may arise within a mediation. At any point, a new Nash equilibrium or focal point may surface, which the mediator can use as an anchor point for an amicable settlement.

Mediation is a unique form of dispute resolution, where the mediator is primed to facilitate the running of the game theory model. Their role here is crucial, as the identification of the game might be the dividing line between an amicable settlement and a withdrawal from the mediation.

https://doi.org/10.1142/9789819801268_0005

Chapter 5

The Role of Negative Emotions in Mediation

Erin Shan Liu

I. Introduction

In mediation, three dimensions of conflict have been identified. These are "the emotional, the cognitive, and the behavioral".[1] For each party, it is the interplay between the emotional and the cognitive that precipitates their behaviour. As such, it is not surprising that mediators are likely to come across various strong, negative emotions during their mediation sessions. In this context, an emotion may be defined as "a felt experience", meaning that one feels the emotion rather than "just think[ing] it".[2] These emotions typically respond to certain stimuli "along with associated thoughts, physiological changes, and a desire to do something".[3]

It is particularly important that negative emotions are "understood" and "effectively addressed" by the parties and the mediator to move towards an amicable resolution.[4] Although the literature on emotion in mediation contexts often portrays negative emotions as a matter which must be managed, diffused, or minimised, current research suggests that negative emotions in and of themselves are not inherently detrimental to mediation and, if skilfully handled, may (1) serve as a tool to facilitate resolution and (2) produce productive behaviour and collaboration between the disputing parties. Instead, it is the negative behaviours that result from experiencing negative emotions which hamper dispute resolution, when emotions are left unaddressed, suppressed, or carelessly handled.

II. The Role Negative Emotions Play in Mediation

A. *Negative emotions as an obstacle to dispute resolution*

Negative emotions are often perceived as being detrimental to the mediation process and in contrast, "consistent, reasoned, objective, and rational decision-making is (the) cornerstone of any dispute resolution process".[5] Although these ideals may be attractive, it is often impossible to completely "separate people from their emotions".[6] Emotions may also be too complex to entirely unpack, but in the context of mediation, mediators may benefit from (1) recognising what may be causing a party's negative emotions; (2) anticipating how this might affect the mediation process; and (3) having a general understanding or developing a framework on how these negative emotions might be managed or even capitalised on in order to facilitate the dispute resolution process.

Negative emotions may hinder mediation by, for example, (1) diverting "our attention from substantive matters"; (2) leaving parties vulnerable to being manipulated; (3) distorting or impairing the parties' reasoning and decision-making processes; (4) fostering "win-lose bargaining" rather than cooperation towards fulfilling the parties' mutual interests; (5) encouraging parties to reject reasonable offers; (6) decreasing the parties' "desire to work together"; (7) causing emotional contagion, stimulating the other party to feel that negative emotion[7]; and (8) causing "tunnel vision" and hampering the parties' "ability to think clearly and creatively".[8] For example, where two parties are parents undergoing a process of divorce and one parent is aroused by anger because he/she feels unappreciated by the other, that parent may lose sight of their common interest in ensuring the well-being of their child and direct a hurtful insult at the other. This may jeopardise the parties' ability to successfully co-parent in the future.

When a party is aroused by a negative emotion, they might "mispredict how they will behave in a cool state".[9] In mediation, when a party is aroused by a negative emotion, they might end up saying or doing something without considering that they might regret their actions later once they have cooled down. A mediator therefore must work to encourage parties to empathise with the future self "who will have to live with" their choices.[10]

Evaluations of past encounters or the recounting of memories may also be biased based on the individual's current emotions.[11] One might under-weigh certain aspects of the experience and over-weigh others.[12] In mediation, if a party is overcome by a negative emotion during their opening statements, it may shape how they recount and evaluate the events surrounding the dispute, under-weighing the positive aspects and possible mutual interests of the parties. However, these evaluations may also impact the party's forecasts about the possibility of future cooperation or resolution with the other party.

B. *Managing negative emotions*

Some researchers agree with the conception of negative emotions as obstacles to a dispute, which need to be managed. Accordingly, multiple frameworks have been created to guide individuals like mediators on how to handle their own negative emotions as well as the parties' negative emotions. The theory here is that achieving an amicable resolution and a smooth mediation process may depend on the mediator's ability to effectively manage how the parties express or manage these negative emotions. However, mediators, in applying these frameworks, often do not appear to focus on minimising the magnitude of these negative emotions or dampening them. Mediators, after all, are not therapists. Rather, the focus is often on modulating and managing the external behaviour of the parties and how the parties express or interpret their negative emotions.

1. *Emotional intelligence*

Daniel Goleman's conception of emotional intelligence (**"EI"**) is often promoted as a framework for managing emotions during mediation.[13] EI is defined as "the capacity for recognizing our own feelings and those of others, for motivating ourselves, and for managing emotions well in ourselves and in our relationships".[14] Goleman breaks down this definition into a list of skills which are indicative of an individual's EI: (1) self-awareness, (2) self-management, (3) social awareness, and (4) relationship management.[15] The literature on mediation suggests that the management of negative behaviour, stemming from negative emotions, which hinders the mediation process, might be better achieved by mediators who are able to develop these skills and apply them to the mediation. Additionally, mediators should consider developing their EI as well as aiding the parties in developing the listed competencies during the mediation as research has found that parties "experience more positive mood and satisfaction when negotiating with an emotionally intelligent counterpart regardless of how they perform financially".[16]

Self-awareness is described as "the ability to read one's own emotions and recognize the role that those feelings might play in decision-making".[17] For example, a mediator who is angry after being stuck in traffic for a couple of hours should be aware and acknowledge such emotions. It is important for a mediator to be aware of these negative emotions so that he/she might avoid projecting them onto the parties.[18] Emotional outbursts on the part of the mediator may undermine the perception of objectivity and neutrality, trust, and possibly the parties' confidence in the mediator's competence. A mediator should gauge his/her own comfort level regarding emotional expression in general and his/her feelings about the conflict at hand as this may affect the mediator's reactions and behaviour.[19] The mediator should subsequently also promote emotional self-awareness, possibly by encouraging the parties to reflect on their "tolerances for expressing feelings".[20]

Self-management is "the ability to control one's emotions and impulses and to adapt to changing circumstance".[21] In the mediation context, this requires that the mediator "minimize the effect of" his/her "negative emotions while leveraging the impact of positive emotions".[22] A mediator should especially note that he/she should avoid suppressing negative emotions (whether it be one's own or that of the parties) like anger, annoyance, or resentment as it may impair his/her ability to effectively mediate the dispute. In this regard, research suggests that (1) negative emotions will continue to persist regardless of one's efforts to suppress them; (2) this may lead to increased tension; and (3) suppressing an emotion will take up "cognitive energy", a finite resource, which should be directed towards resolving the substantive issues of the dispute between the parties.[23]

Social awareness is known as "the ability to sense, understand, and react to other people's emotions while comprehending social networks".[24]

When a party expresses negative emotions and the reasoning behind such emotions during mediation, a mediator should demonstrate that he/she empathises with the parties to the dispute. This can be done, for example, by saying "I hear that this is very upsetting to you. Can you tell us more about it?". Empathy also involves active listening, which requires that the mediator not "just listen to the words but the ambience that surrounds them, to listen for the mood, character, atmosphere... emotional tone that put the words into a context" — the "meta-messages" — and read the parties' body language.[25] Active listening allows a mediator to develop a better understanding of each party's communication style, so that a mediator may reframe a party's statements in a way that (1) avoids miscommunication; (2) reframes the statement in a more constructive manner; and (3) clarifies the party's interests and objectives to the other party.

Finally, relationship management "is the ability to inspire, influence, and develop others while managing conflict".[26] Negative emotions might result in behaviour which will hurt the relationship between the parties, hamper collaboration, and decrease the likelihood of the parties maintaining a working relationship in the future. An emotionally intelligent mediator should therefore be able to manage behaviour and ensure the parties are able to cooperate in resolving their dispute.

2. *Core concerns*

Alternatively, Fisher argues that dealing directly with emotions, as one does under the EI framework, may be too time-consuming and particularly challenging where the mediator would "also need to spend time thinking about each person's differing views on substantive issues and the process for working together".[27] According to Fisher's framework, mediators should instead focus on appropriately meeting the "five core concerns" which may be responsible for the negative emotion.[28] These include (1) appreciation; (2) affiliation; (3) autonomy; (4) status; and (5) role. These core concerns act "as a lens to understand the emotional experience of each party" and a "lever to stimulate positive emotions".[29]

Expressing appreciation requires that the parties' "thoughts, feelings and actions are acknowledged as having merit".[30] Where parties do not feel that they are being appreciated, this may lead to negative emotions such as anger. A mediator could prevent negative reactions by understanding the party's point of view, "find[ing] merit in what they are thinking, feeling, or doing", then "communicat[ing] the merit [they] see".[31] These first two steps might be achieved through active listening, acknowledging how the party feels, and validating those feelings.

However, Schreier takes this further by proposing that "anger serves the cognitive function of alerting us when others place insufficient weight on our welfare".[32] Thus, a party to mediation might be looking for something more than appreciation and might require that the other party place sufficient weight on that party's welfare and express appropriate concern about the same.

Building affiliation means that the parties should feel they are treated and treat each other as colleagues instead of adversaries.[33] This factor is particularly important as it is self-perpetuating. Being treated as an adversary would cause a party to be angry, but anger can also cause individuals to "act" as adversaries by assigning blame and perceiving "that others are responsible for negative events".[34] To manage negative emotions such as resentment, fear, or anger, the mediator might choose to conduct the mediation in a more informal manner, emphasise the common interests of the parties, or ensure both parties have an equal opportunity to speak.[35]

Respecting autonomy involves each party respecting the other's "freedom to decide important matters".[36] Negative emotions such as frustration might arise because a party feels that their autonomy is being disrespected. In mediation, one may ensure autonomy is respected by consulting the parties before deciding on issues such as the agenda or whether to move on to the next stage of the mediation process.[37] In this regard, it may also be essential that mediators not prescribe the outcome for the parties.

Lastly, acknowledging status describes where parties' standing is given full recognition, and choosing roles is when the parties feel that they have a defined role that they find "fulfilling".[38] These aspects may be achieved by ensuring both parties get an equal chance to convey their views.

However, particularly strong negative emotions may lead to rash behaviour like charging out of the mediation venue or back-and-forth yelling. This might significantly hinder the process of reaching settlement.

For such cases, Fisher suggests multiple tactics such as taking a break[39] or facilitating an apology between the parties. Breaks may be of particular help as, in such cases, emotions which are suddenly stimulated are often "short-lived", facial "expressions are fleeting, and physiological responses quickly fade".[40]

C. *Negative emotions as facilitative and a tool to reach resolution*

Although much of the literature on mediation focuses on "managing" expressions of negative emotions, psychological research suggests that these negative emotions could sometimes be used to facilitate or benefit mediation.

The expression of negative emotions gives the mediator as well as the other party a better understanding "about core concerns, underlying interests, and hidden barriers to agreement".[41] Indeed, emotions have been conceptualised "as communication systems that help people navigate and coordinate social interactions by providing information about others' motives and dispositions".[42] This subsequently helps parties decide whether "to pursue cooperative or competitive strategies with" the other.[43] Thus, genuine expression of negative emotions such as anger may, in certain contexts, aid mediation as anger "signals a desire for behavioral adjustment" and may prompt the other party to adopt "more cooperative strategies".[44]

However, mediators should be aware of how the expression of certain negative emotions may be received by the other party in different contexts. Under some circumstances, expressing negative emotions may encourage empathy and collaboration in achieving a mutually beneficial resolution. However, anger will likely not be effective when communicated by those who are in a lower power position; for instance, an employee expressing anger towards his boss may backfire and cause the boss to reciprocate that anger.[45] In such cases, it may be better for a party to express disappointment rather than full-fledged anger as it "engenders more cooperation", regardless of whether the party is of a higher or lower power position.[46]

Thus, when mediators encounter certain negative emotions during mediation, it is important that they recognise its communicative function and that they help the parties communicate their feelings in a manner that promotes cooperation and avoids misinterpretations. However, mediators should also ensure that the emotions being expressed are emotions which the party is genuinely experiencing and be wary of encouraging a party to express negative emotions which might manipulate the other. This is especially essential in the mediation context as "whether discrete emotions are judged as authentic or contrived may influence their impact on economic and relational outcomes".[47] A party who believes the other is feigning a negative emotion is unlikely to want to cooperate with the other party.

It has also been argued that experiencing a negative emotion such as stress and the "physiological changes that co-occur" with such stress is "not necessarily bad".[48] Instead, negative emotions may "energize" parties "to work toward reaching agreement".[49] That is to say, mediators can develop techniques such as reappraisal which "reduces self-reported negative feelings in response to negative events".[50] Accordingly, if the "physiological arousal experienced during" a situation which elicits a negative emotion is reframed "as a resource that aids (and enhances) performance", the target individual will experience more positive outcomes.[51] Reappraisal includes telling a target individual that "signs of physiological arousal (e.g., increased heart rate) that accompany (stressful) situations predict better, not worse, performance".[52] Therefore, a mediator could encourage parties aroused by frustration to channel this into motivation to resolve the situation precipitating the negative emotion.

However, some research claims that reappraisal may not always be effective and instead suggests using one negative emotion "to alter another", a process which requires "less cognitive effort and control" from the target individual.[53] Specifically, "sadness induction could reduce aggressive behavior associated with anger".[54] Although using a negative emotion like sadness to modulate another emotion (e.g., anger) might not be viewed as a desirable solution for the party, it might at least prevent aggressive behaviour or behaviour which seriously threatens the resolution of the dispute. For example, in a mediation which involves friends who have fallen out due to the dispute and one party is being hostile towards the other party, the former party could be made to reflect on their loss of friendship, thereby inducing sadness. This may counteract the anger that the party harbours towards the other. However, a mediator should be cautious in inducing negative emotions in this manner as it raises possible ethical issues and veers towards manipulation.

Furthermore, affect is defined as "a feeling that something is good or bad".[55] Although only considered "a faint whisper of emotion", researchers have highlighted the important role of affect experienced during decision-making and assessment of risk,[56] which might be essential in a mediation.

For example, statistics which are framed in terms of probability may have less impact than those framed in terms of frequency.[57] One study found that 41% of professional psychiatrists refused to discharge a patient if they were informed that out of every 100 patients similar to the target mental patient, 10 were estimated to commit an act of violence against others (the "**frequency condition**"). On the other hand, only 21% refused to discharge the patient if they were informed that patients similar to the target patient had a 10% chance of committing an act of violence against others (the "**probability condition**").[58] These results were explained to be because of affect. Specifically, psychiatrists in the probability condition experienced "relatively benign images of one person unlikely to harm anyone", whereas psychiatrists in the frequency condition reported that the representations created frightening images of violent patients (e.g., "some guy going crazy and killing someone").[59] Therefore, when mediators frame or reframe statements by removing negatively charged language or language which provokes negative imagery, this may affect the party's assessment of risk and influence decision-making.

By using affect, mediators may even elicit negative emotions to highlight to the parties the undesirability of their alternatives. Although risk and benefit are typically positively correlated in practice, people often perceive them to be negatively correlated.[60] This is because "people base their judgements of an activity not only on what they think about it but also on how they feel about it".[61] Therefore, if an individual's feelings regarding a particular activity are favourable, he/she will likely judge the risks of that activity to be low and the benefits to be high. Moreover, if someone provides that individual with information about the disadvantages of that activity, this will lead to a negative overall affect and the individual would perceive the risks of the activity to be high.[62] Such a phenomenon might explain why reality testing a party's alternatives is an effective strategy in encouraging the party to settle the dispute in mediation. If a mediator highlights the disadvantages of litigation such as the costs, losses to time, or inconvenience involved, the party will subsequently feel negatively about this alternative and feel more compelled to settle the dispute during mediation. Alternatively, if the highlighted disadvantages and risks of litigation are perceived to be serious enough, they may elicit negative emotions such as fear, thereby encouraging settlement between the parties.

III. Conclusion

Ultimately, insufficient research has been conducted on the advantages of negative emotions in the mediation context to be conclusive. However, general research on negative emotions demonstrates that negative emotions may not be inherently detrimental to mediation and mediators may in fact use these negative emotions to facilitate the mediation process.

https://doi.org/10.1142/9789819801268_0006

Chapter 6

Investigating Neighbour Disputes and Mediation in Singapore through Behavioural Economics to Foster Stronger Communities

Li Kelun

I. Introduction

With around 80% of the Singaporean population living in public housing administered by Singapore's Housing and Development Board (**"HDB"**),[1] disputes between neighbours are inevitable. Noise, unacceptable conduct, and obstructions to, or misuse of, common corridors were the top three causes of neighbour disputes mediated in 2022.[2] Crucially, neighbour disputes have been on the rise since the COVID-19 pandemic.[3] For instance, the monthly average of noise complaints made to the HDB grew eightfold from 400 in 2019 to 3,200 in 2021. Although the number decreased to 2,300 a month in 2022 and 2,150 a month in 2023,[4] the overall upward trend remains concerning. The increase in the number of neighbour disputes necessitates more instances of mediation and therefore ensuring the success of mediation is crucial, such that these warring disputes can be peacefully mended before further damage is done to the harmony of the community.[5]

In this chapter, the different reasons for the need for mediation in neighbour disputes and how mediation can resolve these issues to varying degrees of effectiveness are first discussed briefly. Then the factors that render mediation ineffective in certain situations are explored in detail, drawing upon insights from behavioural economics. Finally, several approaches that mediators can employ to mitigate the adverse effects of cognitive biases to contribute to building a stronger community are presented.

II. Reasons for Mediation in Neighbour Disputes

A. *Ineffective communication*

The HDB advises residents affected by neighbour disputes to communicate with their neighbours politely, listen to them and be willing to compromise before approaching the Community Mediation Centre (**"CMC"**).[6] However, effective communication may not be practised by the affected parties since the common causes of neighbour disputes can easily generate a sense of frustration for the affected party, translating into emotionally charged confrontations towards the other party. Such harsh, non-emphatic messaging may leave recipients defensive[7]; a defensive or resistant recipient can result in a dismissive approach, disregarding the feedback provided.[8] Hence, the breakdown in communication causes the dispute to be unresolved by the two affected parties alone, necessitating the intervention of a third-party mediator to facilitate discussions. In this case, the dispute can be resolved relatively easily with the help of a mediator who facilitates positive communication between the parties. Mediators at the CMC define the issues in conflict, clarify the parties' positions and interests and guide the parties towards resolution.[9]

B. *Difference in cost–benefit evaluation of settlement*

The respective parties in the dispute will most likely agree to a settlement if they perceive it to be more beneficial than the alternative of non-settlement, such as escalating the case further to the Community Disputes Resolution Tribunals (**"CDRT"**) in Singapore, which will incur legal costs as well as large amounts of their time.

However, a settlement may not happen when one of the parties views the benefits and costs of settlement significantly differently from the other party, inducing the party to refuse to settle as they perceive that the costs of doing so outweigh the benefits. Consequently, the dispute can become much more complicated to resolve due to cognitive biases that influence how the person views the dispute, which will be explained in detail in the following section.

III. Cognitive Biases in Neighbour Disputes: Why do Different Parties View the Same Situation So Differently?

Before investigating the different economic biases, it is useful to first understand how mediation can take place ideally between two perfectly rational economic agents.

A. *The economic model of dispute resolution*

The ideal situation of mediation can be analysed with the standard economic model of human behaviour exemplified by the *homo economicus*, the portrayal of humans as ideal decision-makers with complete rationality.[10] During the mediation process, both parties will communicate and gauge the maximum amount the respondent is willing to pay or the minimum amount the complainant is willing to accept. These values are known as the reservation values. When the range of the reservation values of both parties overlap, rational economic agents will reach a settlement at any amount in the Zone of Possible Agreement (**"ZOPA"**),[11] which is the zone between the maximum willingness to pay and the minimum willingness to accept, as shown in Figure 1.

However, the assumptions of the *homo economicus* do not hold as the rationality of the two disputants can be notably influenced by the various cognitive biases that will be explained in detail in the subsequent paragraphs.

B. *Endowment effect*

The endowment effect refers to the phenomenon that people often value objects that they own more highly than they would if they did not own them.[12] This can be explained with prospect theory.

Prospect theory is based on the concept of loss aversion, the observation that individuals experience losses more intensely than equivalent

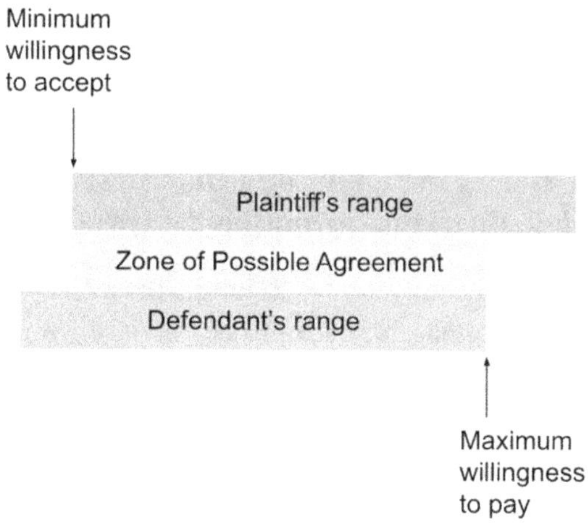

Figure 1. A diagram of the zone of possible agreement.

gains, with research showing that the pain of losing is psychologically twice as powerful as the pleasure of gaining.[13] At its core, the prospect theory revolves around the central idea that the utility assigned to gains and losses by each person is relative to a certain reference point, which is different for individuals and situations.[14] Hence, decisions are made in relativity instead of absolutes, unlike rational economic agents.

Prospect theory posits that the willingness of an individual to give up an object relies on the reference point — whether he owns the object now or not. If he owns it, he will consider the pain of giving up the object. If he does not own it, he will consider the pleasure of gaining the object.[15] However, based on loss aversion, the individual would assign greater value to the pain from giving up the object more heavily than the pleasure of gaining the same object. Since individuals evaluate the options according to their endowed state, they would value the object more highly when they own it.

The endowment effect is not universal and is more strongly felt if the object owned is "for use" rather than "for trade".[16] The effect is more significant for an object that is for personal use or enjoyment than an object that is merely a proxy for exchange with something else of equivalent value. For example, many people would have no qualms about exchanging a $5 note for five $1 coins.[17] However, some people may be extremely unwilling to give up objects that have personal or emotional significance to them.

The endowment effect causes the ZOPA of the two parties involved to be mismatched with little to no overlapping area, making a settlement very intractable, if not impossible, to achieve.

Endowment bias can have a great impact on settlement acceptance, especially when it involves a compromise on one of the parties' personal belongings. For example, in a neighbour dispute involving potted plants cluttering the corridor, the resident may value his potted plants highly as it is a "for use" item and he has put in the effort to cultivate the plants and hence has placed emotional value on his potted plants. The resident is thus likely to be unwilling to remove his plants since there is a gap between the subjective value and objective value of the item in dispute as it is overvalued by the owner compared to the objective value ascribed by the affected party.[18] The mismatch prevents an agreement from being made, where both parties are unable to reach a consensus as the resident who owns the potted plants feels that the cost of giving up his potted plants is far greater than the utility gained from the removal of his potted plants, such as improved corridor accessibility.

C. *Reactive devaluation*

Reactive devaluation refers to the observation that the offer of a particular proposal or concession may diminish its apparent value or attractiveness in the eyes of the recipient.[19] In the 1991 study conducted by Ross and Stillinger,[20] a sidewalk survey was administered to assess participants' positions on a mutual reduction of arms by the US and the Soviet Union. Respondents were asked to evaluate the terms of a nuclear disarmament proposal — a proposal that the interviewer ascribed, depending on experimental conditions, to the Soviet Union, to the US, or to a neutral third party. Unsurprisingly, the American respondents viewed the terms of this plan as unfavourable to the US when the Soviets were the putative originator, while the same terms appeared moderately favourable when attributed to a neutral third party and quite favourable when attributed to the US.

Reactive devaluation can occur for a few main reasons. One reason is the fear of incomplete information. During mediation, both parties may worry that the opposing side has undisclosed information that could give them an advantage. Hence, when an option is offered by the opposing side, the receiving party could suspect that the option is biased and that the offering party has a hidden goal which is concealed in the offer.[21] This leads to the mentality of "they would not have made the offer if those terms did not advance their own interests more than mine",[22] resulting in the offer being quickly dismissed.

Another reason is that the respective parties view the dispute as a zero-sum game, in which any gain achieved by the other side is perceived to be a loss, of equal magnitude, to their own side — so that the very idea of a mutually advantageous trade of concessions becomes a psychological, if not a logical, impossibility.[23] This is especially prevalent when there are high levels of enmity between the two parties. In the context of neighbour disputes, this can be likely when disputes with "neighbours from hell" result in feelings of distrust and hostility, preventing the parties involved from judging proposals objectively.

In other cases where hostility is not present, reactive devaluation can still occur due to a change in underlying preferences.[24] Human beings seem inclined, in various circumstances, to reject or devalue whatever is freely available to them and to covet and strive for whatever is denied them, even when no hostility is perceived.[25] The saying "the grass is always greener on the other side" encapsulates this source of reactive devaluation, where the constant desire for an even better alternative causes individuals to prematurely dismiss the plan.[26] This happens because one could interpret the suggested option as a signal that the opposing party is now willing to yield and make concessions to reach settlement and that, if pushed further, the offering party may make further concessions.[27] Such tactics, however, can lead to unnecessary deadlocks, delays or failures to discover efficient outcomes.

This may be particularly relevant in Singapore due to its unique *kiasu* culture, where the fear of losing out on an even better opportunity potentially causes proposed solutions to be dismissed prematurely.

The consequence of reactive devaluation is that the ZOPA becomes narrower, making a settlement that is agreeable to both parties harder to achieve.

D. *Optimistic overconfidence*

Optimistic overconfidence refers to people's tendency to have overly optimistic predictions about events that may arise in the future.[28] Although this is only part of a more general phenomenon of humans placing unwarranted confidence in their predictions,[29] it is also highly applicable in the field of dispute mediation as disputants tend to overestimate the prospects for prevailing in the absence of a negotiated settlement.[30] The optimism bias can make it challenging to achieve an amicable resolution in the dispute. The defendant's reservation value would be lowered due to optimism bias, while the reservation value of the plaintiff would become higher, which would lead to a narrower ZOPA or even to its disappearance.

One factor at play is asymmetric information. In disputes, each side tends to have more complete information about their own goals, assumptions, and agenda compared to the opposing side.[31] Additionally, the availability heuristic comes into play, where people are prone to judge a given situation based on their personal experiences or on the basis of immediately available information, consequently giving too much weight to these experiences and information when making decisions.[32] In neighbour disputes, there will unavoidably be differences in experience for the same subject matter, especially when it is of detriment to one side and benefit to the other. For example, in a neighbour dispute over loud music, the resident might disagree with the claim that he is in fact being inconsiderate by playing loud music frequently as he preferentially recalls the instances where he was not playing music, incorrectly concluding that he rarely plays loud music and thereby perceiving the complaining neighbour as being unreasonable. Hence, he would perceive reaching a settlement as disadvantageous for him.

Another relevant phenomenon is the self-serving bias, where people tend to conflate what is fair with what benefits oneself.[33] Referring back to the example of loud music, the resident who is playing loud music regards the experience as beneficial as he can enjoy listening to his music. Hence, due to the biases in experience, judgments based on this biased experience or information may well be equally biased. As a result, disputants fail to account for gaps in knowledge, causing their decision-making to be biased.

This results in stalemates during negotiations and creates an impasse. If negotiators estimate the value of the alternatives to negotiated settlements in self-serving ways, this could rule out any chance of settlement by eliminating the ZOPA.

IV. Proposals for Mediation in Neighbour Disputes

While a facilitative approach can be effective when both parties are open-minded, a more active approach adopted by the mediator may be required to resolve disputes that are heavily influenced by these various cognitive biases. As such, the mediator should try to eliminate the potential for biases to influence the decision-making process with the proposals described in the following sections.

A. *Greater mediator involvement in negotiations*

Mediators can play a crucial role in mitigating perhaps the most damaging cognitive bias, reactive devaluation, as it can be present in both parties and can lead to the discussion between disputants deteriorating into an acrimonious one.

As aforementioned, reactive devaluation causes the proposal offered by the other side to appear less attractive because of its authorship. Hence, mediators can circumvent this bias by removing the element of authorship to make the proposal more attractive to the recipient,[34] such as offering the proposal on behalf of the party. Alternatively, the mediator can practise "shuttle diplomacy", where the mediator acts as a middleman between the parties, facilitating communication without direct interaction between the parties themselves. This can be accomplished during the private sessions, where mediators at the CMC speak to parties privately.[35] In doing so, the mediator can discover what each side is willing to compromise and then facilitate a proposal that incorporates these concessions. With the mediator as the author of the proposal and attributed to neither party, reactive devaluation can be diminished as both sides perceive the mediator as trustworthy, with no vested interest in the outcome of the negotiation.

This approach encourages both parties to voice out their concerns and evaluate the proposal, allowing them to be more willing to compromise and maximise joint gains.[36] Additionally, this makes it feasible for disputants to make concessions with reduced risk of losing face; the things that each side may be reluctant to give to the other, which might have been interpreted as signs of weakness, may now be ceded in response to the proposal.[37] This is especially relevant in Singapore, where face is a quality embedded in Singapore culture.[38]

Additionally, mediators can also protect disputants from the optimistic overconfidence bias by offering their own opinions. Potential litigants are likely to adopt more realistic assessments once a disinterested third party has examined the contentions and evidence from both sides and rendered his or her opinion about the "settlement" value of the case.[39] Hence, mediators can help disputants to be more objective in their assessment of the chances of successful negotiation.

B. *Effective framing*

Framing is the way a communicator defines and constructs any piece of communicated information, which affects the choices people make about how to process that information.[40]

Effective framing is vital in ensuring a smooth mediation process as it can help change the perspective in which the disputant parties view the conflict, resolving the cognitive biases that have impeded them from viewing the conflict objectively. Hence, it is paramount for the mediator to create an environment that allows both parties to construe specific proposals and concessions in a constructive manner, which can be attained with the effort of the mediator to frame the discussion in a manner that is conducive to successful negotiations. The mediator's framing of the negotiation can turn the parties' attention away from the concerns with equity or fairness to the pursuit of self-interest or group interest.[41]

To limit the endowment effect, mediators can frame the discussion in such a way that reduces the inhibiting effects of loss aversion, a key factor contributing to the bias. During discussions, mediators can choose to highlight the costs associated with the conflict-laden status quo, making a settlement seemingly more favourable when such costs are taken into account.[42] Mediators can also employ semantic framings or labels that lead the parties to perceive the negotiation in positive terms, making the benefits of settlement more salient to both parties to encourage them to be more willing to reach a compromise.[43] For example, when handling neighbour disputes, the mediator can frame the discussion as improving neighbourliness as well as emphasising the negative impacts of how non-settlement affects both parties, such as a cluttered walkway being a serious potential fire hazard and hampering life-saving efforts during emergencies.

The power of framing effects is exemplified in a 1993 experiment conducted by Liberman *et al.*[44] Around 48 Stanford undergraduates were divided into two groups to play the famous Prisoner's Dilemma Game, where a player can either defect to maximise their own outcome at the expense of the other player or cooperate for a lower personal gain but greater overall gain for both players. The key difference between the groups was that the game was referred to as the "Wall Street Game" in one group and the "Community Game" in the other. The results exhibited that the construal manipulation of naming the game differently had a huge impact on the subjects' decision, with more than two-thirds of the "Community Game" group cooperating, while only one-third of the "Wall Street Game" group chose to cooperate, showcasing how even a simple change in the name of the game can elicit greater trust between players and encourage greater cooperation.

Mediators can further lessen the tendency for the parties to view their concessions as losses by inducing them to perceive the things they will be giving up as "bargaining chips" or "negotiation currency" that can be readily exchanged.[45] This is helpful as the endowment effect is less prominent when the object given up is viewed as "for trade" rather than "for use", as explained earlier.

V. Conclusion

In short, this paper highlights the relevance of incorporating behavioural economics into the field of mediation through the analysis of several key cognitive biases that cause mediation to fail. Additionally, this paper also offers some suggestions for mediators to eliminate the effects of these biases for the true effectiveness of the mediation process to be realised. Nonetheless, it is important to acknowledge that the CMC has a commendable settlement rate of 80%,[46] and the author hopes that this research paper can promote further increase in the settlement rate, helping to build a stronger and more harmonious community.

https://doi.org/10.1142/9789819801268_0007

Chapter 7

Learning through Competing: The Pedagogical Value of Mediation Competitions in Mediation Education

Muhammad Syazwan Bin Ramli

I. Introduction

Mediation competitions have become increasingly prevalent in introducing law students to mediation as a mode of dispute resolution and may even be seen as a complementary aspect of mediation education in law schools today. Mediation competitions typically run as extracurricular endeavours in addition to conventional mediation courses in universities, which ordinarily consist of classroom theory lessons and practical role-play exercises.[1] Mediation competitions today are largely organised by educational institutions, mediation training institutes such as the International Academy of Dispute Resolution (**"INADR"**), non-governmental organisations such as the International Chamber of Commerce Paris (**"ICC Paris"**), and are often sponsored and supported by law firms. In these mediation competitions, short of honing their mediation skills in live mediation sessions in legal practice, students are provided the opportunity to practice their mediation and mediation advocacy skills in a relatively low-stakes environment through the simulation of mediation scenarios in a competition setting.

It may thus be said that mediation competitions play an important role in mediation pedagogy because they represent a mode of education and skills training that is an alternative to "traditional" classroom settings. Mediation competitions also inherently carry great value in enriching the skills of law students by providing them with cross-cultural experiences, due to factors such as the cultural diversity of participants in international competitions, and the ability to interact with participants who have been exposed to diverse training methodologies and mediation education pedagogies.[2]

In this chapter, the following pedagogical benefits of integrating mediation competition participation in mediation education to law students are explored and analysed: (1) skill development; (2) cultural exposure; and (3) promotion of mediation as a field of academic interest. The manner in which the skills developed by law students in mediation competitions can better equip them for mediation careers post-graduation will also be explored.

II. Skill Development

A key component of conventional mediation education is the use of role-plays. Indeed, a survey of more than 130 mediation teachers participating in a mediation pedagogy conference hosted at Harvard University found that 96% of the survey respondents used role-play "very frequently" or "frequently".[3] This is because such role-plays have been found to perform the following functions[4]:

1. enhance student motivation and interest in mediation;
2. enhance students' concept learning, decision-making skills, and systematic analytical skills;
3. improve future course work;
4. trigger affective learning of the subject matter by changing students' perspectives and orientations, and increasing their empathy and appreciation of others' circumstances;
5. enhance participants' self-awareness and self-confidence; and
6. promote better student–student and student–teacher relations.

Thus, participation in mediation competitions can be viewed as a potentially valuable aspect of mediation education given that mediation competitions use role-plays and simulations as the primary "vehicle for participation and assessment".[5] Further, through mediation competitions, mediation pedagogy can be tested and developed in two ways.

Firstly, participants of mediation competitions would be able to refine their mediation skills through exposure and practice, and secondly, mediation instructors themselves may be able to refine coaching techniques and contribute to the growth of a community of mediation instructors. These points emphasise the value of mediation competition participation in mediation education, playing an important role in mediation pedagogy.

The refinement of participants' mediation skills through participation in mediation competitions arguably stems from the structure and nature of such mediation competitions. Preliminarily, the *de facto* competitive nature of such mediation competitions improves the effectiveness of any mediation training and education provided in preparation for such competitions, given that students expectedly become "more committed to competition activities than they do to standard classroom exercises".[6] It is this level of motivation and commitment that has been found to lead to the "resulting intensity and quality of … negotiations, to be typically much higher than in the classroom setting".[7]

In terms of structure, mediation competitions generally comprise several rounds in which different cases or role-plays are mediated. To facilitate these role-plays, general instructions as well as simulated confidential information documents are distributed to the teams prior to the competition. From these documents, students are expected to parse the information therein and develop a mediation strategy, and in competitions such as the FDI Mediation Moot, participants must submit a written mediation plan prior to the competition's start,[8] ensuring that student participants explicitly flesh out key elements, such as the parties' positions, interests, and alternatives, in order to formulate a cogent mediation strategy.

Students are also provided exposure to the different roles that exist in a mediation, which typically encompass the mediator(s), the parties to the dispute (also known as "clients"), and their legal counsel (also known as "mediation advocates"). In this respect, some competitions, such as the INADR International Law School Mediation Tournament, allow students to rotate through all these roles, providing opportunities for participants to gain exposure and build a deeper appreciation and familiarity with all three roles. Further, competitions such as the ICC Paris International Commercial Mediation Competition provide student participants with the opportunity to participate in mock mediations mediated by a professional mediator, thereby gaining exposure in that regard. Outside of such competitions, it may be rare for students to access opportunities to observe how professional mediators conduct mediation sessions.

Mediation competitions also provide opportunities for participants to be exposed to a variety of mediation scenarios. In this respect, mediation competitions may themselves be conducted thematically, focussing on disputes of a particular nature. For instance, the International Investor-State Mediation Competition (IIMC) organised by The Moot Court Bench based in Sri Lanka focusses on allowing student participants to build their knowledge and skills in Investor–State Mediation. Alternatively, these mediation competitions may include role-play scenarios requiring the discussion and settlement of matters in various areas of law (such as cross-border commercial mediation, family mediation, and victim–offender mediation). For instance, the 2022 edition of the University of Central Florida Conciliator Mediation Tournament, run in accordance with INADR rules, set mediation role-plays against the backdrop of (1) a parental abduction scenario, (2) an employment dispute, and (3) a negligence suit. These examples go to show the breadth and depth of knowledge and exposure that students stand to gain, depending on the nature of the competition in which they participate. In contrast, given constraints as to the structure and duration of law school mediation courses, law students may not be able to receive this breadth of exposure through university lessons alone.

Aside from the potential educational benefits stemming from the structure of mediation competitions, students crucially stand to develop hard skills that are essential to effective mediation. These hard skills may be evinced through the competitions' judging rubrics, which provide a framework of skills and abilities that participants are expected to train, develop, and be able to replicate in competition rounds. These rubrics include the following[9]:

(1) Preparation, which encompasses aspects such as analysis of the problem, explication of the interests of all parties to the mediation, and development of a mediation strategy;
(2) Process, which encompasses aspects such as flexibility, communication, effective teamwork, listening skills, empathy, the ability to move

toward a collaborative outcome without giving up one's own commercial interests and needs, and the ability to collaborate and be creative in option generation; and

(3) Outcome, which encompasses aspects such as the deliberation of options agreed upon to assess value creation and interest preservation, self-analysis, and ethical behaviour.

Students are thus expected to expend time to develop their skills in these aspects and may thereby develop these skills more rigorously, potentially surpassing the skill development they may receive through the role-play training from their university's mediation courses alone.

III. Cross-Cultural Exposure

There are also pedagogical benefits in the cross-cultural element of mediation competitions. A key part of mediation competitions, and particularly those of an international nature, is that participants ordinarily hail from different cultural backgrounds. In this respect, "culture" may be a difficult concept to define, given that approaches to cultural difference are often based on "tribal culture, ethnic culture, or national culture", leading to concepts of national character that can be reductionist, essentialist, and non-dynamic.[10] Regardless, this difficulty can be reconciled with the understanding that it is nevertheless "possible to formulate concepts of cultural difference, and differences between national systems and people of different nationalities" given that different countries have different legal, educational, and structural frameworks which continue to "influence the values people hold and the way they think".[11] As such, where there exists the mixing and confluence of student participants from across the world in mediation competitions, there will inevitably be cultural differences and therefore cross-cultural exposure. In the context of mediation pedagogy, it is submitted that the most crucial cultural difference resembles the diversity in negotiation and mediation styles of different participants. Such cultural diversity would be "difficult, if not impossible, to reproduce" in classroom settings where negotiation styles are likely to be much more homogeneous because classmates are more likely to have been educated in the same tradition" and may hail from similar national, socioeconomic, and educational backgrounds.[12]

Mediation competitions therefore allow students and even their accompanying instructors to be exposed to differing approaches to mediation of participants from different cultures, traditions, and diverse educational backgrounds. When students are confronted with negotiators from other cultures, it may influence their negotiation demeanour and strategy in aspects such as lexical choice, choice of framing, and even the way they convey any legal threat as part of their mediation strategy. For instance, where a team of students from a common law jurisdiction negotiates against another team of students from a civil law jurisdiction, there may conceivably be differences in the way they formulate and express their legal position, and the way they attempt to comprehend the legal position of the other party. The cruciality of this difference is underscored by the importance of understanding the other side's legal position even in mediation, notwithstanding the nature of interest-based mediation which prefers to look past strict legal technicalities, given that an understanding of such legal positions directly impacts the BATNA of each party. Thus, such opportunities for exposure are "invaluable for the participating students because they help them understand the "effect" of their personal negotiation style(s) in different settings and constellations".[13]

Even for mediation coaches and instructors, mediation competitions can provide good opportunities for networking and sharing teaching strategies and approaches. This exchange of ideas, when considered together with the opportunity for these instructors to watch their approaches in action when their students participate in the competition's rounds, allows them to "optimize their existing teaching approaches and methods and also encourages them to try new ones".[14]

A criticism may be made of the alleged cross-cultural value of such mediation competitions, which is that such competitions promote cultural imperialism, particularly that of Western culture, instead of promoting the proliferation of cultural diversity. In this regard, a salient manifestation of this cultural imperialism is arguably seen in the fact that mediation competitions typically hold the American negotiation model of interest-based mediation as a normative standard, where the guidelines and score sheets used by judges are "based largely on concepts that can be directly traced back to Roger Fisher and William Ury's seminal book Getting to Yes

(1981)".[15] As such, where the interest-based model of mediation is the *de facto* model to which participants are expected to adhere and by which they are thereby judged, there is an imposition of Western values that subverts genuine cultural exchange of different cultural approaches to mediation within such competitions. Indeed, it has been said that "cultural differences that can have crucial impacts on conflict resolution argue against any universally valid model — interest-based negotiation or any other".[16]

Nevertheless, it is argued that concerns of "Westernism" through the primacy of the interest-based model of mediation do not undermine cross-cultural exchange and exposure. This is because this model has, in praxis, been "exported all over the world by teachers, trainers, and practitioners",[17] where its primacy has transcended American (or "Western") shores. For instance, the Singapore Mediation Centre "combine[s] the Harvard model of interest-based negotiations with a unique understanding of cultural nuances necessary in mediating disputes in Asia"[18] in its training courses and uses this model as a standard for its accreditation processes. As such, mediation competitions allow participants (and coaches) to be exposed to diverse approaches to the same model, allowing for the development of mediation pedagogy through the refinement of current approaches and the adoption of useful innovations.

Further, it is submitted that this criticism raises a pertinent point for the further development of mediation pedagogy, that mediation education and competitions may expand to include "alternative", non-Western conceptions of mediation. For instance, given that competitions can be organised to favour a certain style of mediation through their structure and judging rubrics, it means that competitions based on models different from interest-based negotiation can also be organised (although this has yet to become prevalent). There is thus ample opportunity for the discovery of alternative approaches to mediation, such as the informal alternative dispute resolution practices in Muslim communities, China, Japan, and Africa, as well as those of "communitarian" societies whose "traditional indigenous practices" have led to "significantly different expectations about how mediators and disputants might behave".[19] Interest and awareness of these different conceptions of mediation can be built through cultural exchange at competitions or even through "alternative mediation" competitions, alongside formal education and training of the same through university courses.

IV. Promoting Mediation as a Field of Academic Interest

Another way in which mediation competitions can contribute to the advancement of mediation pedagogy is through the increased awareness and attention to mediation as a dispute resolution mechanism. Indeed, this consciousness of mediation can help lead to the development of a community of young mediators and mediation advocates involved in the mediation competition circuit. Further, the increased attention to mediation competitions can encourage academic institutions to invest greater resources in mediation training and education for their students.

In the context of student negotiation competitions, it has been said that given that many student negotiation competitions are organised by academics passionate about negotiation, such competitions often take place at these academics' universities. This helps promote negotiation as both "an academically interesting topic and as a key skill useful in private life and professional careers". Further, such competitions also increase student interest in "attending negotiation courses, emphasizing the role of such courses in academic curricula, and helping secure the resources necessary for conducting negotiation research at the host institution".[20] It thus follows that with more resources, greater time and effort can be invested into mediation research, expanding the field of mediation academia and developing more robust mediation pedagogy.

A. *Preparing students for careers in mediation*

Aside from the mere development of mediation pedagogy, it is arguable that a primary motivation for having robust mediation pedagogy in the first place is to stand mediation-educated students in good stead to embark on professional careers in mediation. In this respect, mediation competitions can complement this aim to boost such professional motivations by providing student participants with opportunities to network with suitable professional connections and to amass the skills needed to develop mediation as a professional aspect in their careers. However, mediation-educated law students who eventually graduate and want to practice mediation in general may find it difficult to formally break into the professional mediation scene, given that they "lack real-world legal experience that mediation participants expect in a mediator".[21] In this respect, mediation competition participation is nevertheless important, given that the mediation education and training required to eventually take on mediator roles is well provided through participation in mediation competitions. For instance, it has been observed at competitions such as the ICC Paris International Commercial Mediation Competition that student participants were able to engage in transformative mediation as the "norm, rather than the exception",[22] by focussing on important aspects of mediation like relationship building and collaboration to find mutually beneficial solutions to the parties in mediation. Such observances show that students who participate in mediation competitions can "rapidly acquire" the skills and techniques that are "necessary to be effective mediators",[23] and perhaps the gap remaining to be filled would be that of experience.

One way that law students may be able to fill that experience gap is to continue participating in such mediation competitions to build competence as well as to build a network of peers and mentors in the mediation scene. These mentors may be able to provide guidance as to how to prepare and develop oneself for mediation practice and may even be good sources of opportunity for co-mediation or observation of mediation sessions.

Further, students with mediation competition experience and developed mediation and mediation advocacy skills may find it easier to successfully acquire professional mediation accreditation. This is especially so where such accreditation programmes are selective and limited and such competition experience may be able to provide students with the edge to set them apart from their peers. For instance, in Singapore, the Intellectual Property Office of Singapore (**"IPOS"**) runs the Young IP Mediator Initiative (**"YIPMI"**) where it appoints a small number of students each year, providing these selected students with the "opportunity to participate in the mediation of a real-life IP dispute, as well as other projects related to the field of Intellectual Property mediation".[24] Such appointments are good ways for young practitioners to build up their mediation portfolio early on, therefore underscoring the importance of participating in mediation competitions to be able to be equipped with the requisite skills to grasp opportunities whenever they arise.

V. Conclusion

Regardless of whether or not mediation competitions are effective vehicles for the development of mediation pedagogy, it is undeniable that such competitions are a hub for both students and practitioners across the world to gather. Such competitions thus offer excellent opportunities for students to network and make new connections, identify interests and passions in the world of law, and generally challenge themselves and stretch their horizons, and should thus be encouraged. Ultimately, mediation is more than just a legal dispute resolution mechanism — it is a way of life, and the skills and values it carries are worth impressing upon as many persons as possible, and in as many ways as possible, including through competition.

https://doi.org/10.1142/9789819801268_0008

Chapter 8

Contemporary View on the Legislative Improvement of Mediation and Mediation Technologies in Socially Relevant Areas in Russia

Natalia Kharitonova

I. Introduction

In recent years, there has been a growing interest in the use of mediation and mediation technologies as a means of dispute resolution in Russia, particularly in various socially significant areas of practice.

The resolution of conflicts through mediation is founded on a philosophical and theoretical basis that is quite different from conflict resolution through litigation, with party self-determination as an essential feature.[1] A mediator assists in conducting a dialogue, facilitating the establishment of contact between the parties, the formation of the sphere of true interests, and the development of an executable solution. The legislative improvement of mediation in Russia began in the 2000s when the first federal law on mediation was adopted. Relations associated with the application of such a procedure to disputes arising out of civil, administrative, and other public relations, such as those related to entrepreneurial and other economic activities and disputes arising from labour relations and family legal relations, are regulated by Federal Law No. 193-FZ of July 27, 2010 "On Alternative Procedure of Mediated Dispute Resolution (Mediation Procedure)"[2] (the **"Federal Law No. 193-FZ"**).

II. Scope and Development of Mediation in the Russian Federation

Federal Law No. 193-FZ, effective as of January 1, 2011, creates legal grounds for the emergence and development of mediation in the Russian Federation and is a practical step towards the implementation of mediation procedures envisaged by the Federal Target Programme. A significant motivator for the introduction of mediation procedures in the Russian legal system was the need to regulate issues arising out of the introduction of compulsory conciliation procedures in the resolution of certain types of disputes.

Given the fact that any law requires periodic changes, updates, or replacement, discussions on such improvement of the legislation governing mediation in Russia have been going on for several years. Nowadays, there are active discussions and debates concerning the drafting of a new law on mediation in Russia, and such discussions are widely debated at the governmental level.

At present, the institution of pre-trial dispute resolution, such as mediation, is underdeveloped in Russia. This is due to a lack of significant legal practice and late legislative attention. At the same time, there is a wealth of experience in the application of mediation procedures in other foreign countries, the study of which will improve and allow for the successful application of mediation in Russia.

The variety of possible scenarios for the application of mediation does not imply the possibility of legislating a prescribed procedure for the implementation of mediation. Such a procedure is usually determined by the mediator based on the circumstances of a particular dispute, the position of the parties, as well as the opinion of the mediator himself (in the absence of unified training standards, the mediator community is divided into several conceptual directions, each of which has its own vision of the optimal procedure of mediation).

From the point of view of legal regulation, mediation can be divided into pre-trial, trial, and post-trial mediation.

The scope of Federal Law No. 193-FZ is defined as applying to the settlement of disputes arising from civil relations, including those related to entrepreneurial and other economic activities, as well as to the settlement of disputes arising from labour and family relations. Mediation may be carried out at any stage of court proceedings, as well as without recourse to judicial authorities.

It should also be noted that the provisions of Federal Law No. 193-FZ also do not apply to situations of conflict resolution and making amends in criminal proceedings and proceedings relating to cases of administrative offences (restorative mediation). In this regard, certain undertakings of restorative mediation remain outside of legislative regulation and often depend solely on the goodwill of the parties involved.

Thus, the application of mediation in Russia goes beyond the scope of existing legal regulation, and thus a harmonious development of the institution of mediation is possible only with the improvement of relevant legislation.

In 2019, significant amendments were made to Federal Law No. 193-FZ, the result of which is that a mediation agreement reached by the parties as a result of a mediation procedure conducted without referring the dispute to a court, if notarised, has the force of a writ of execution. Thus, a notarised mediation agreement has acquired the status of an enforcement document along with a notarised alimony agreement or a notary's certification. This change should contribute to a popularisation of dispute resolution through mediation, the result of which will satisfy both parties' interests and needs.

III. Principles of Mediation under Federal Law No. 193-FZ

Mediation is carried out on the basis of certain principles enshrined in Article 3 of Federal Law No. 193-FZ, among which principles such as (1) confidentiality, (2) impartiality and independence of the mediator, (3) voluntariness, and (4) cooperation and equality of the parties are highlighted.

A. *Confidentiality of mediation proceedings*

Under Federal Law No. 193-FZ, confidentiality shall be maintained with respect to all information obtained and indicated in the course of the mediation procedure. Federal Law No. 193-FZ stipulates separately that a mediator may not disclose information which became known to him as a result of the mediation procedure. In this respect, the mediator may disclose information that he became aware of in the course of negotiations only with the consent of the party that provided such information. At the same time, the mediator shall warn the parties in his introductory speech before the start of negotiations that he cannot guarantee non-disclosure of information obtained by the parties, thereby relieving himself of responsibility for any possible subsequent disclosure of information.

The mediation process maintains confidentiality during negotiations, which is crucial for certain parties involved. The discussions are limited to the mediator, the disputing parties, and possibly their representatives. To preserve confidentiality, no stenographic, audio, or video recordings are allowed during the mediation process. Any notes taken are destroyed once the negotiations conclude, emphasizing the importance placed on maintaining the privacy of the discussions.

B. *Mediator independence and impartiality*

The principle of mediator independence is a fundamental one in dispute resolution via mediation. Mediators in civil, family, or labour disputes are independent persons who do not side with any of the parties and do not suggest solutions to resolve the conflict. Their main task is to guide the parties to a solution that satisfies the interests of both parties.

C. *Voluntariness*

Voluntariness in the mediation process means that all parties enter into the negotiation process voluntarily, and the mediator is freely chosen by the parties.

D. *Equality of parties*

The principle of equality of the parties enshrines the equal position of the parties in negotiations, and neither party may compel the other to do anything. Neither may the mediator, by his or her actions or words, put one party in an advantageous position or take sides. The mediation process is designed to maintain equality, with the mediator first hearing the positions of each party separately before facilitating mutual negotiations between them, ensuring both parties are given equal attention and consideration.

IV. Applicability of Mediation and Areas for Reform

Despite the fact that mediation is an alternative method of dispute resolution, its application cannot be universal because mediation must be applicable to the dispute. The legal components of applicability of mediation include the following:

1. The will of the parties to settle the dispute through mediation;
2. The category of the dispute being one which can be resolved by mediation;
3. The agreement reached by the parties in mediation only affecting the interests of those persons involved in the mediation process;
4. The parties' authority to enter into a mediation agreement;
5. The possibility of procedural registration of the mediation outcome.

At the same time, law enforcement practice has revealed a number of shortcomings in Federal Law No. 193-FZ, including the following:

1. An extremely low threshold of entry into the mediator profession and the complete absence of mediator training standards or basic requirements for such professional development programmes;
2. A lack of accounting and control over the activities of mediators and organisations that provide mediation services;
3. A lack of separate requirements for mediators in potentially sensitive areas of mediation such as family mediation with the participation of young children;
4. A lack of a coordinating state body in the application of mediation procedures.

As a consequence of these gaps in legislation, the market for mediation services has been saturated with mediators with extremely low qualifications, leading to a general discrediting and underdevelopment of the institution of mediation in Russia.

Further, changes in legislation, such as the recognition of notarised mediation agreements as having the force of an enforcement document, have provoked the formation of a vicious practice of unfair use of notarised mediation agreements for the purpose of illicit trafficking and cashing, as well as for other fraudulent schemes.

In order to create favourable conditions for the development of mediation procedures in the Russian Federation and further popularisation of such methods of alternative dispute resolution, the Ministry of Justice of Russia proposed, among others, the following changes for consideration at parliamentary hearings held in April 2023:

1. The introduction of mandatory federal standards for mediators and organisations that provide mediation;
2. The creation of a state information resource or registry containing information on mediators, organisations involved in providing mediation procedures, and accredited educational institutions for the professional training of mediators;
3. The establishment of a procedure for obtaining the right to provide mediation services;
4. The streamlining of procedures for the professional training of mediators and their accreditation;
5. The establishment of special requirements for mediators carrying out their activities in socially significant areas of practice;
6. The definition of cases for the mandatory referral of parties to an initial consultation with a mediator before proceeding to court;
7. The introduction of a mechanism for the monitoring of the activities of mediators and mediation service providers.

A. *Qualification requirements for mediators*

In accordance with Federal Law No. 193-FZ, mediation can be carried out on a professional and non-professional basis. Under Article 15 of Federal Law No. 193-FZ, persons who have reached the age of eighteen, have full legal capacity, and do not have a criminal record can perform the functions of a mediator on a non-professional basis. In contrast, professional mediators are persons who have reached the age of twenty-five, have a higher professional education, and have completed a training course under the training programme for mediators approved in the manner established by the Government of the Russian Federation (Article 18 of Federal Law No. 193-FZ).

The activities of non-professional mediators are proposed to be abolished in the new law on mediation in Russia, since insufficiently qualified provision of mediation services may lead to issues in the execution of settlement agreements reached during the mediation process.

At present, persons who have reached the age of twenty-five, have a higher education, and have received additional professional education on the application of the mediation procedure, as well as retired judges, can carry out the activities of mediators on a professional basis. However, as practice shows, compliance with these criteria is insufficient to guarantee the provision of mediation services of a satisfactory quality. The mediator needs to have a wide range of knowledge and competencies to facilitate effective dispute resolution in various areas of law. Thus, current requirements for advanced training programmes for mediators appear insufficient and ill-equipped to provide a satisfactory level of mediator training.

It should be noted that, in 2019, Federal Law No. 193-FZ was amended to provide that mediation agreements certified by a notary have the force of executive documents. However, since this amendment, cases of abuse of the right and use of notarised mediation agreements for the purpose of illegal circulation and cashing of funds have become increasingly prevalent.

It seems appropriate to establish separate requirements for mediators operating in socially significant areas of practice, such as family mediation involving minors, school mediation, and inheritance disputes involving minors. Special attention should be paid to equipping these mediators with skills and knowledge to discuss and prevent destructive situations from occurring.

For the successful implementation of these proposals, it is necessary to develop standards for the training of mediators and special educational programmes in this area, as well as to streamline the procedure for the professional training of mediators.

Further, matters relating to the establishment of requirements for organisations to ensure the proper conduct of mediation and the supervision of such organisations remain outside the scope of current legal regulation. Thus, measures establishing a procedure to obtain the status of a mediator, increase the accountability of providers of low-quality mediation services, and introduce a mechanism to admit organisations that ensure the provision of mediation services of satisfactory quality are required.

B. *Register of mediators*

Federal Law No. 193-FZ provides for the creation of a register of self-regulated organisations in the field of mediation. The power for the creation of this register is entrusted, in the absence of an authorised state authority in the field of mediation, to the Federal Service for State Registration, Cadastre, and Cartography. However, the creation of this register has not been forthcoming, seemingly due to the lack of responsibility and practical significance.

Therefore, the creation of a unified federal register, which includes information on mediators and organisations engaged in activities to ensure the proper conduct of mediation, will help to organise information on the number of mediators, facilitate the search for suitable mediators by citizens and the process of sending parties to mediation, and increase public awareness of mediation. The presence of a mediator in the unified federal register in the field of mediation will serve as additional confirmation of his professional qualifications.

For ease of navigation, mediators and organisations providing mediation services can be categorised based on their area of expertise over certain types of disputes (for instance, economic disputes, family disputes, disputes involving minors, and conflicts in educational institutions).

Also, within the framework of the unified federal register in the field of mediation, a further possible proposal could be to include the accounting and registration of educational and training institutions engaged in the training of mediators.

V. Conclusion

In conclusion, based on the above-mentioned discussion, some recommendations are made to improve the institution of mediation in Russia:

1. A comprehensive development of legislation in the field of mediation with the definition of a public authority authorised to carry out the functions of developing and implementing state policy and legal regulation of mediation should be considered;
2. Relevant federal executive authorities should consider the possibility of raising standards and requirements relating to the professional training of mediators and the development of specialised educational and training programmes for socially significant areas of practice;
3. Separate requirements should be established for mediators involved in mediation and reconciliation services in educational institutions, as well as for the accounting and registration of such mediators.

Thus, the legislative improvement of mediation and mediation technologies in socially significant areas of practice in Russia is an important step towards creating a more efficient, accessible, and fair legal system. The new law provides a solid legal basis for the development of the mediation profession, promoting the use of mediation technologies and ensuring greater transparency and accountability within the mediation process. As mediation continues to gain popularity in Russia, it is likely to become an increasingly important tool in resolving disputes in various areas of society.

https://doi.org/10.1142/9789819801268_0009

Chapter 9

Resolving Drama with a Trauma-informed Approach in Family Mediation

Sebastian Hoe Wee Kiat

I. Introduction

Drama is defined as any situation or series of events having vivid, emotional, conflicting, or striking interests or results.[1] This chapter will explore the family drama that is highly emotional and conflictual for the various actors involved. Specifically, this chapter will focus on the context of marital drama and the actors therein.

The dramatis personae involved may have suffered traumatic experiences in their childhood and in their interactions with each other. Some examples would include family violence or adverse childhood experiences. When these persons end up as parties in mediation, the mediator must ideally be equipped with knowledge to conduct mediation with a trauma-informed approach with a view to resolve the drama.

This chapter is based on academic research and the author's professional experience working as a Family Social Worker while studying at the Singapore University of Social Sciences, School of Law (Juris Doctor programme). This chapter is structured to provide ease of understanding of the following matters:

- Why a trauma-informed approach is necessary in family mediation;
- What drama entails;
- How trauma may affect the actors of the drama;
- Actors in a family mediation;
- How a trauma-informed approach can apply to family mediation; and
- Vicarious trauma and self-care for mediators.

Family Mediation is unique as opposed to commercial mediation. Commercial disputes may include matters such as breach of contract, intellectual property disputes, or other claims such as loss of profits. Commercial mediation typically involves having lawyers present and working out a way to resolve the business dispute at hand. Commercial interests are at the heart of commercial disputes.

This is opposed to family disputes and family mediation. While there may be a business relationship involved in the dispute, there is an additional element of familial intimacy, given that nothing is more intimate than family relationships where family members typically eat, sleep, and play together and generally live in the same household.

Family mediation is special because the interpersonal relationships involved are highly important. Families are typically viewed as forming the fundamental bedrock of our society. Family relationships such as marital relationships involve both the husband and wife working together to advance their mutual benefit. In the Singapore context, the law even demands that married couples safeguard and advance their marital union. For instance, in Singapore, section 46 of the Women's Charter 1961 provides the legal demand for married couples to safeguard their relationship as "an equal cooperative partnership of their different efforts for their mutual benefit".

However, like all relationships, married couples face challenges and may argue throughout the lifetime of their marriage. When married couples are able to resolve their marital disputes, their arguments possibly do not raise serious issues for the relationship. However, such arguments become an issue when married couples are unable to resolve their marital disputes. This is where a mediator with knowledge of trauma-informed approaches to mediation could provide necessary assistance to mediate and bring resolution to the marital drama.

II. Why a Trauma-Informed Approach Is Necessary in Family Mediation

A trauma-informed approach to family mediation is essential given that family mediation involves family disputes that are highly emotional with the possibility of the parties involved having faced traumatic experiences in their life.

Firstly, the knowledge of a trauma-informed approach to mediation would allow the mediator to resolve the drama of the dispute in a professional and evidence-based manner. The mediator, being a neutral party, would be able to use social science in mediating the dispute of the parties, which is likely to be highly conflictual and emotional.

The mediator would be able to identify possible signs and symptoms of trauma exhibited by the parties and would have a better understanding of why such parties are responding in a certain way. The mediator could then craft and facilitate a strategy to create a safe space to allow the parties displaying strong emotional behaviours to openly discuss their concerns. This could help create the best possible environment to assist the parties in coming to a resolution.

Secondly, a trauma-informed approach to mediation matters because it is consistent with good ethical practice. Family disputes ordinarily involve potentially vulnerable clients who may or may not trust the mediator fully. Nonetheless, the mediator has a duty to conduct himself or herself ethically.

The mediator could face ethical dilemmas when the clients share information with the mediator during the mediation session. For example, if there are allegations of serious child abuse or imminent risk of harm to the parties involved, the mediator has an obligation to inform relevant external parties or authorities to ensure the safety of the persons at risk of harm. This is an exception to the general confidentiality of mediation.

Therefore, the knowledge of a trauma-informed approach would bring better awareness to the mediator in identifying the potential signs and symptoms of family violence. The mediator could resolve the drama while preventing himself from breaching any code of conduct or laws in the respective jurisdictions.

III. What Drama Entails

Past trauma can also cause current drama. Imagine a situation where a Social Worker, employed in a Family Service Centre to help families resolve their emotional and family issues, encounters a transnational couple who had married in Singapore walking into the Family Service Centre and seeking social support. The husband is Singaporean and the wife is Vietnamese. Even after two years of marriage, the couple is still reliant on rental housing. This causes the wife to become unhappy with the husband as she feels that the husband is unable to provide a stable housing arrangement for them as they have little choice but to share the rental apartment with the other tenants. They have arguments from time to time because of this issue. One day, out of frustration, the wife brandishes a kitchen knife at the husband during an argument. The police are called in and a stern warning is issued to the wife.

Subsequently, both husband and wife are referred by the police to a Family Service Centre for family counselling and support. The husband shares that he is doing his best to provide for the family and is traumatised by the wife's act of intimidation by brandishing a knife. The wife appears apologetic and cries during the family session with the mediator. She shares that she is stressed at that moment, but she loves her husband. The husband shares that he finds it difficult to explain his situation because he believes that men cannot be victims of family violence. Relatedly, society often attaches stigma to family violence and those suffering from traumatic experiences. A trauma-informed approach to mediation would allow for a better understanding of these complexities, facilitating more effective resolution of family disputes.

According to a Special Report on Nonfatal Domestic Violence in 2003–2012 by the Bureau of Justice Statistics of the United States Department of Justice, only 1 in 9 men have experienced severe intimate-partner physical violence as compared to 1 in 4 women.[2] Society, in general, is heavily skewed towards interpreting family violence as against women. The reality is that victims of family violence can be both men and women.

It is true that not all drama includes violence or trauma. However, a mediator needs to be aware of what the drama entails and the possibility of trauma and family violence involved.

A. *Definition of family violence*

The terms "Family Violence" and "Domestic Abuse" may be used interchangeably. However, it is crucial for mediators to understand the various terms involved amidst the drama of family cases. The distinction between these two terms relates to the relationship between the offender and the victim.[3] In the case of Domestic Abuse, it involves the individual committing abuse towards an intimate partner, whereas in the case of Family Violence, it involves a family member committing violence against another family member.

The United Nations defines domestic violence[4] as "a pattern of behaviour in any relationship that is used to gain, or maintain power and control over an intimate partner". In the Singapore context, the current definition of family violence can be referenced under section 64 of the Women's Charter 1961, where Family Violence is defined as causing hurt to a family member, placing a family member in fear of hurt, wrongfully confining a family member against his or her will, and/or causing continual harassment.

There had been changes to the Singapore laws to enhance protection for family violence victims. The Women's Charter (Family Violence and Other Matters) (Amendment) Act 2023 was passed by Parliament on 4 July 2023.[5] The changes would define family violence more broadly. Family violence would cover a wider range of acts such as sexual abuse, emotional abuse, and psychological abuse. Such abuse can be found either through a single instance or through a course of behaviour.

B. *Definition of trauma*

According to the American Psychological Association,[6] trauma is an emotional response to a terrible event such as an accident or natural disaster.

Social science and psychology have provided us with some theories to understand the possible responses to trauma by a victim. A mediator with basic knowledge of how humans respond to trauma would be able to better resolve the drama of family mediation.

IV. How Trauma May Affect the Actors of the Drama

There are typically four responses manifested by individuals when faced with a threat. In this context, trauma is one such threat that individuals may face, and individuals typically respond to trauma through the fight, flight, freeze, and/or fawn responses.[7] The fawn response is a relatively new research addition to the field of psychology.[8] Mediators will be well equipped in the session when they are aware of these possible responses to trauma.

A. *Fight response*

Under the fight response, the individual would respond to the threat with conflict. Fight respondents believe that they will gain control of their situation if they establish power over the threat. This response will provide an adrenaline rush to the individual defending himself through fighting, shouting, and controlling others. The individual's thought process is focused on the need to eliminate the threat before the threat eliminates him.

Common behaviours of fight respondents could include the following:

- Crying;
- Tight fists indicating the desire to punch;
- Tight jaw and grinding teeth; and
- Feelings of anger and rage.

B. *Flight response*

Under the flight response, the individual would respond to the threat through escape. The individual's thought process is focused on running away from the threat.

Common behaviours of flight respondents could include the following:

- Fidgety behaviour or feelings of tenseness;
- Feelings of bodily restlessness, shown through actions such as the constant movement of legs, feet, or arms; and
- Feelings of anxiety, shown through actions such as shallow breathing.

C. *Freeze response*

Under the freeze response, the individual would respond to the threat through disassociation. The individual's thought process is focused on not doing anything so that the threat cannot hurt him.

Common behaviours of freeze respondents could include the following:

- Stiffness and heaviness;
- Holding one's breath or restricted breathing;
- Feeling stuck, frozen, or numb;
- Increased heart rate; and
- Feelings of dread.

D. *Fawn response*

Under the fawn response, the individual would respond to the threat through placation. Fawn respondents avoid or deal with conflict through "people-pleasing". The individual's thought process is focused on appeasing the other party so that the individual can be safe from conflict or pain.

Common behaviours of fawn respondents could include the following:

- Neglecting one's own needs;
- Pretending to agree with the other party;
- Being overly apologetic to the other party;
- Finding it difficult to say no to the other party's suggestions;
- Excessively flattering the other party; and
- Being overly accommodating to the other party.

V. Actors in the Family Mediation

In a typical family mediation for married couples in heterosexual relationships, there are three actors. The husband, the wife, and the mediator. The next section of this chapter will explore how mediators can work with the husband and wife to resolve their dispute through knowledge of a trauma-informed approach to mediation.

VI. Definition of Trauma-Informed Approach

The trauma-informed approach assumes that an individual is more likely than not to have experienced trauma in their lifetime.[9] It recognises the symptoms of trauma and acknowledges how trauma can affect an individual. This also includes how trauma can affect mediators through vicarious trauma.

There is a paradigm shift in the approach that Mediators can utilise in the trauma-informed approach. Instead of asking themselves questions like "What is wrong with this individual?", mediators practising a trauma-informed approach to mediation would instead ask themselves "What has happened to this individual?". Mediators would look into understanding what exactly had happened to the husband and wife, instead of placing fault on either party.

The purpose of the trauma-informed approach is not to resolve the symptoms of trauma faced by the individual, as that would be better resolved by a trained counsellor. The purpose of the trauma-informed approach is to provide mediation services in a way that is appropriate and accessible to individuals who have experienced trauma.

This also relates to good ethical practices as family mediators should seek to resolve family disputes without exacerbating trauma symptoms. It would be unethical for a mediator to resolve family disputes but at the huge expense of re-traumatising the individuals involved.

VII. Applying the Principles of a Trauma-Informed Approach

There are five principles of the trauma-informed approach, namely, Safety, Choice, Collaboration, Trustworthiness, and Empowerment.[10] These principles generally do not distract from the usual goals of mediation. In fact, these principles are aligned with the principles of effective mediation.

A. *Safety*

Mediators need to ensure the physical and emotional safety of the parties involved in the mediation. This can be done simply by ensuring that the logistical setup of the mediation venue is welcoming and allows the privacy of the parties to be respected. A box of tissues can also be placed within the mediation venue for easy access when needed. After all, a safe space may invite raw emotions and possibly tears during the mediation session.

B. *Choice*

Mediators should inform the mediating parties that they each have a choice to be in the mediation session. The parties to the mediation should be provided with a clear and appropriate message about their rights and responsibilities in the mediation session. For example, it is good practice for the mediator to explain to the parties the purpose and process of the mediation. Family mediation is unique as there may be uneven power dynamics in the family, and the parties may not be familiar with the process of the mediation.

C. *Collaboration*

Mediation is a collaborative process. The mediator serves as the facilitator and guides the parties towards a resolution of their dispute. Both parties to the disputes should be given the opportunity to be heard. They should collaborate as much as possible towards a win-win outcome. Parties should collaborate and consider their Zone of Possible Agreement (ZOPA), Best Alternative to a Negotiated Agreement (BATNA), Worse Alternative to a Negotiated Agreement (WATNA), and options which allow the interests of both parties to be met.[11]

D. *Trustworthiness*

Mediators should inculcate a sense of trust in their work and character. Mediators should ensure that respectful and professional boundaries are maintained, in particular when working with vulnerable clients who have experienced traumatic events in their lives.

E. *Empowerment*

This is similar to the strengths-based approach[12] whereby mediators should prioritise empowering the parties in the mediation. The strengths-based approach focuses on utilising the strengths of the parties involved instead of their deficits to resolve disputes. It is a holistic approach that empowers and promotes the well-being of the parties involved. Mediators could provide an atmosphere where parties to the dispute feel validated and affirmed. This relates to the parties' choice to be present in the mediation session and their ability to openly share their concerns without the fear of being judged.

F. *Therapeutic justice*

A renewed vision for Family Justice in Singapore, known as Therapeutic Justice, is in line with the idea of trauma-informed practice. Family mediation is distinct in that the parties involved flesh out personal family matters in front of the mediator.[13] When the five principles of trauma-informed mediation are aptly applied, a more effective family mediation session is achieved with a higher chance of dispute resolution.

VIII. Vicarious Trauma

According to the British Medical Association,[14] Vicarious Trauma is defined as a process of change resulting from empathetic engagement with trauma survivors. Anyone who engages with survivors of traumatic incidents is prone to be affected by vicarious trauma.

Mediators engaging in a Family Mediation session with trauma involved must thus be aware of their susceptibility to vicarious trauma. The following are some signs of a mediator who may be experiencing vicarious trauma:

- The mediator experiencing lingering feelings such as anger, sadness, and disgust towards the victimisation of the parties to the dispute;
- The mediator becoming emotionally attached to the issue of the dispute or to the parties involved in the dispute to an excessive degree;
- The mediator feeling burnout from work;
- The mediator feeling pessimistic, cynical, and a loss of hope;
- The mediator becoming overly detached and cutting off parties to the dispute when they speak about a traumatic event;
- The mediator having difficulty maintaining professional boundaries with the parties involved, seen through actions such as siding with one

party or doing more than the role of the mediator requires, such as falling in love with one of the parties;
- The mediator feeling like a white knight in shining armour and having rescue fantasies or overly identifying with the parties involved in the dispute. While it is the role of the mediator to be neutral, hear parties out, and assist in resolving the dispute, it is not the job of the mediator to resolve the dispute at all costs. Ultimately, parties to the dispute have the choice and autonomy to mediate.

IX. Self-care for Mediator

Every mediator experiences vicarious trauma differently. Some may not be affected by it, while others may be affected tremendously. There are strategies to reduce the risk of vicarious trauma for mediators. Self-care is vital because mediators can only mediate effectively and take care of other families' disputes when they first take care of themselves. This is also aligned with upholding ethical and professional standards in the field of mediation.

Self-care tips for mediators include the following:

- Maintaining a healthy work–life balance by having hobbies unrelated to work;
- Seeking social support from colleagues, friends, and family members;
- Journaling thoughts and feelings in a diary to help process stressful events;
- Taking up training opportunities related to trauma-informed approaches to mediation;
- Taking time off and scheduling regular breaks as required;
- Keeping physically healthy, such as through proper hydration and adequate exercise;
- Looking after mental well-being by engaging in relaxing and self-care activities;
- Increasing self-observation skills by recognising the signs of stress, vicarious trauma, and burnout; and
- Seeking professional help, such as by seeing a social worker or counsellor if necessary.

X. Conclusion

The disciplines of Social Work, Social Science, and Psychology could provide Mediators in family mediation with a better understanding of trauma and drama in family disputes. The journey towards resolving drama with a trauma-informed approach in family mediation can be challenging.

However, once the mediator is aware of the purpose and benefit of the trauma-informed approach, the mediator can utilise the knowledge to resolve family disputes. The mediator will be guided by the principles of Safety, Choice, Collaboration, Trustworthiness, and Empowerment in providing appropriate mediation services to individuals who may have experienced trauma.

The knowledge of an evidence-based trauma-informed approach could raise professional standards in the field of family mediation while at the same time providing a higher chance to resolve highly conflictual and emotional family disputes. Finally, the mediator needs to be aware of vicarious trauma and provide self-care for himself. The work of the mediators includes dealing with emotional barriers from clients. However, it could also include dealing with the mediator's emotional self.

In conclusion, the mediator needs to address his own emotional issues and prevent burnout before he can excel in the craft of mediation in a sustainable fashion. Drama can finally be resolved with a trauma-informed approach in family mediation.[15]

https://doi.org/10.1142/9789819801268_0010

Chapter 10

How can Artificial Intelligence Assist Mediators: A Technical Analysis

Tristan Koh Ly Wey

I. Introduction

The following is a conversation the author had with ChatGPT, after providing ChatGPT with the facts of a contractual dispute where parties were arguing over the inferior quality of Longans which were delivered late[1]:

Q: Generate 3 ways to reframe the statement "I think the other party is out to cheat me because he gave me lousy Longans".
A: Here are 3 ways to reframe the statement:

1. Can you tell me more about what you mean by "lousy Longans" and how they have impacted your business?
2. What specific terms and conditions in the contract were not met in relation to the Longans?
3. Instead of assuming the other party is acting in bad faith, let's approach this as an opportunity to find a resolution that works for both parties.

ChatGPT seems to exhibit the traits of a competent mediator: First, it conducted active listening by asking the person to share more about what "lousy" meant to him and his business. Second, it established objective criteria to determine whether the Longans were in fact "lousy", such as by reference to the terms of the contract. Third, it reframed pejorative terms like "lousy" and "cheat" by using more neutral terms such as "acting in

[1] This was a mediation exercise scenario created by Prof. Joel Lee.

bad faith", and also suggested shifting towards more productive framing by inviting both parties to share their opinions.

Though *prima facie* mediation seems unlikely to be easily automated by Artificial Intelligence (**"AI"**) because mediation requires sensitivity to emotion and awareness of linguistic nuances, ChatGPT seems to have such capabilities as demonstrated. ChatGPT is an eminent Generative Pre-trained Transformer (GPT) that appears to have taken natural language processing (NLP) capabilities to the next level. This brings up the question as to how current state-of-the-art AI can assist mediators. AI that assists mediators can bring about multiple benefits, such as increasing efficiency in resolving low-complexity mediation disputes and thereby increasing access to justice. For instance, in 2002, eBay implemented an automated online dispute resolution (ODR) solution that targeted disputes below a certain quantum. This ODR solution now handles over 60 million disputes annually.[1] Though the original solution did not use AI, eBay demonstrates that the right kind of technology with the right implementation can effectively handle low-level disputes. Hence, with an increase in the performance of AI, it is worth investigating how AI can be used to assist mediation. In particular, this chapter will focus on how AI utilising "human-in-the-loop" systems can be used to assist mediators. Under this model, the mediator retains full control over the process and AI provides additional information which helps the mediator make better decisions.[2] Though there can be higher levels of AI-assisted mediation, current technology is unlikely to be able to automate the mediation process to such an extent.

This chapter seeks to show, from a technical perspective, that current AI can assist the mediator with regard to two skills: emotional communication and creativity. These skills are commonly thought to be poorly modelled by AI because they deal with unquantifiable thought processes that do not have any fixed patterns.[3] However, it is submitted that advances in technology make it possible for AI to reach some appreciable level of competency in these skills. In particular, deep learning is much more effective in dealing with unstructured data like representations of emotions, and creative processes intrinsic to generating solutions can be algorithmically modelled to optimise for Pareto-optimal outcomes.

II. The Role of AI in Mediation and Dispute Resolution

Preliminarily, the requirements of AI used for adversarial dispute resolution such as litigation and AI used in non-adversarial settings such as mediation must be distinguished.

AI used for mediation should have very different capabilities compared to AI used for litigation. For instance, AI used in adversarial processes is frequently used to predict legal outcomes. The AI's performance metric is whether the AI would have produced a decision similar to how a human judge or arbitrator would have decided the case.[4] The goal of AI then is to train machine learning models that can sufficiently model legal argumentation. However, mediation is less about predicting outcomes and more about facilitating the process of problem-solving between the disputing parties. Facilitative mediation is defined as clarifying and enhancing communication between the parties to help them decide what to do.[5] In this regard, AI for mediation should be geared towards encouraging communication between the parties, with the broad performance metric being not whether the AI achieves the same resolution as the human mediator but whether the parties felt there was genuine communication and cooperation. Of course, such a metric is less objective and measurable than the case of AI used for adversarial dispute resolution, but this metric can be broken down into more objective components, such as measuring the emotional state of parties before and after an AI-mediated session. Nevertheless, as Riskin argues, there is a spectrum of mediation styles, and the goal of evaluative mediation could be the same as that of predicting legal outcomes, like how AI is used to predict legal outcomes in litigation. Furthermore, some functions of AI that deal with process automation can be similar across the modes of dispute resolution. For example, document management software used for litigation can easily be used for mediation as well since both relate to categorising legal documents.[6] However, this chapter will only discuss AI that can be used for substantive mediation instead of process automation.

A. *AI and emotional communication in mediation*

First, AI should have the capability to understand emotions and communicate in an emotionally sensitive manner relevant to the context of the dispute. Reframing is one such technique that can be used. Being emotionally aware is important throughout the mediation, as emotion both motivates and prohibits parties from coming to an agreement.[7] The most powerful interests are basic human needs such as a sense of belonging or control over one's life.[8] If these needs are not met, they create fear or anxiety in the parties. Conversely, if these needs are met, they create calmness or confidence. The mediator facilitates communication between the parties by detecting and interpreting such emotions. This facilitation helps parties to share their respective interests that underlie their positions. While no AI can completely replace a mediator's emotional awareness, AI is also not as emotionally apathetic as one might think. Like probabilistic algorithms that can detect patterns, AI can be trained to recognise similarities in text, voice, or facial expressions that relate to emotional communication.

To this end, deep learning is a significant breakthrough for emotion recognition as it overcomes the limitations that were prevalent in classical machine learning. Datasets used to train machine learning models for emotion recognition are in the form of unstructured data and are highly multi-dimensional. For classical machine learning models to be trained on such data, time and computationally intensive techniques must be used for feature engineering and selection. This makes such models impractical to use in mediation sessions where emotions need to be detected in real time. Deep learning overcomes these limitations through its model architecture, which makes emotion recognition technology more practicable for deployment.[9]

One experiment used deep learning techniques to predict the outcome satisfaction of negotiation and how much the negotiating partners liked each other from the text conversation of their negotiation. A combination of deep learning models was able to identify seven types of emotions based on the plain text and the emoticons used by the participants, and these emotions were highly correlated with self-reported scores of negotiation satisfaction and partner likeness.[10] Therefore, AI that recognises emotional states can help mediators ask more relevant questions to facilitate communication between parties. This could be especially useful since most communication is non-verbal[11] and relies on the subjective perception of the mediator himself who is also influenced by their own emotions and prejudices.[12] Further, emotional intelligence includes self-awareness and self-management of the mediator's own emotional state.[13] Therefore, AI that acts as an "objective" observer without any emotional prejudices of its own could provide the mediator with enhanced emotional intelligence since the mediator can compare his own intuitive observations of the parties with that of the AI to gain a different perspective of the issue.

Beyond emotional recognition, communicating in an emotionally sensitive manner is another component of emotional intelligence. As mentioned earlier, ChatGPT seems already able to generate context-sensitive text responses that reframe emotionally laden statements. Deep learning models have also been trained to generate emotionally sensitive text. One model was able to generate text responding to different types of emotions (e.g., anger, sadness, joy), intensities, and topics (e.g., politics or technology).[14] Though these models have general use cases and topics, it is a proof of concept that current state-of-the art AI can both recognise emotion and respond in an emotionally calibrated manner. Nevertheless, these are still separate AI models with very specific capabilities. A general model close to exhibiting emotional intelligence has not been created yet. AI that is able to substitute parts of the mediator's job is still some ways off due to the complexity of combining different specialised subsystems that themselves perform at a reasonable level.[15]

One concern is whether there are suitable datasets available to train models specifically for mediation. This challenge is especially pertinent considering that communication is culturally specific as how emotion is expressed and perceived varies widely across cultures. For example, Japan has a much higher aversion towards uncertainty compared to Denmark.[16] In this case, Japanese parties compared to Danes could be much more reluctant to express contentment with a mediator who may not be so structured in facilitating the mediation. Hence, models that were trained on emotions observed in a Japanese context may not be as effective when used in Denmark. Therefore, mediation AI should be tailored to the specific culture to ensure that the training dataset captures different cultural factors.

Further, another consideration is whether AI will ever achieve emotional intelligence despite advances in technology. Though AI may be trained to recognise emotions and even generate text that is emotionally aware of the dispute, ultimately parties want to be affirmed for their values and views. Out of the five emotional concerns which were identified as being critical towards addressing emotions during mediation, appreciation and affiliation require the creation of a relationship between the mediator and the parties.[17] Further, regardless of outcomes, there is higher reported satisfaction from face-to-face alternative dispute resolution (ADR) compared to ODR.[18] This requires direct human interaction, which AI will never (or be very unlikely to) replicate.

B. *AI and creative problem-solving in mediation*

Creativity should be another capability of mediation AI. Mediators help parties generate options for mutual gain based on their BATNA (best alternative to a negotiated agreement). These options are intended to fulfil the parties' interests rather than positions.[19] As it is probably impossible to fulfil both parties' original positions, the mediator helps the parties look beyond these positions to generate solutions that can fulfil both parties' interests instead. This process requires much creativity because as opposed to adversarial dispute resolution, the issue is not framed as a simple distributive issue of who gets the larger portion of the pie, which is usually about the distribution of scarce, quantifiable resources such as money.[20] This process of finding mutually beneficial solutions seems like an intractable problem because, first, there is no defined, fixed procedure to find the best solution. It all depends on how the parties react to the mediator and to the other party during the session. Second, positions and interests are sometimes non-quantifiable, which would prevent a computer from understanding the problem space.

However, there are AI methods that could overcome these challenges. One of the benefits of AI is that it can provide workable solutions to problems that are computationally intractable. For example, AlphaGo, a computer programme created to play the board game Go, has successfully defeated human Go players by using a random tree search algorithm to find moves that were previously learnt using neural networks. Though the algorithm does not exhaustively search through all the possible moves to find the best move, the algorithm provides moves that have increased AlphaGo's performance beyond that of human Go players.[21] Hence, even if not all challenges stated here have been fully addressed, AI can still help to produce satisfactory solutions.

The first method which can be used to overcome the challenges is to formulate a solution generation process algorithmically. An algorithmic expression of a problem brings the problem one step closer to being computationally solvable. This is as opposed to a non-algorithmic problem such as whether it is morally right for the state to mandate that all passengers in cars must wear seatbelts because there are no defined steps to follow to arrive at an answer. One algorithmic expression of the problem has been proposed in the following[22]:

1. Give advice on respective BATNAs (i.e., what would likely happen if the mediation fails);
2. Attempt to resolve any existing issues using argumentation or dialogue techniques;
3. For issues not resolved, deploy compensation / trade-off strategies to generate solutions;
4. If parties are not satisfied with the solutions, return to step two and repeat the process recursively until either the parties are satisfied or agree to stop the mediation.

Second, in relation to compensation/trade-off strategies in step two, optimising for Pareto-optimal solutions could be one possible strategy used by the mediation AI. Pareto-optimality is defined as a situation where it is impossible to make someone better off without making someone else worse off. For example, suppose that two neighbours have a dispute regarding a tree that is a part of both of their properties. Neighbour A wants the tree removed because it blocks his view, while Neighbour B wants to keep the tree because it provides him with shade. A Pareto-optimal solution could be that they agree to leave the tree as it is so that B still gets the shade, but both would take turns to trim the branches on A's side so that A's view would not be obstructed. With this arrangement, doing anything more to the tree would make either A or B worse off and is therefore Pareto-optimal. Of course, this is not the only Pareto-optimal solution. Perhaps another solution would be for them to agree to remove the tree, but A could pay 50% of the cost of constructing a shelter for B's house. As AI algorithms are designed to optimise for a particular target, an algorithm could be designed to optimise for Pareto-optimality. Some researchers have done so, by first categorising the issue to be solved as continuous (distribution of money) or discrete (whether the tree is removed). Depending on the type of issue, different algorithms are used to solve for Pareto-optimal outcomes.[23] In some other AI models, an algorithmic mediator is used to help the parties achieve Pareto-optimality and uncover the parties' preferences.[24] Importantly, these algorithms are computationally efficient and function under incomplete information.

Outside of academic discourse, SmartSettle is a proof of concept of mediation and negotiation AI, having been commercially available since 2011.[25] SmartSettle Infinity, the most advanced solution with the ability to provide multi-issue support, requests parties to assign numerical values to each issue to indicate its importance to each party and satisfaction ratings to indicate their best- and worst-case scenarios (i.e., BATNA and WATNA). Parties can indicate equivalent swaps such as Issue 1 – Option A + Issue 2 – Value X = Issue 1 – Option B + Issue 2 – Value Y, which provides a proxy for SmartSettle to gauge the parties' preferences. SmartSettle is then able to generate different options of equivalent satisfaction, even if they were not originally proposed by the parties. SmartSettle can therefore be effective at quickly resolving issues that are easily reducible to quantifiable, discrete issues. However, SmartSettle may not sufficiently capture the problem space of more complex issues, as it forces parties to assign numerical values to options that may not necessarily be quantifiable. A farcical but demonstrative example of relying on a purely quantifiable approach is Solomon's proposed "solution" to cut the baby in half to solve the problem of two women both claiming that the baby was theirs.[26] However, AI can still supplement the mediator's creative problem-solving by using the human-in-the-loop system, mitigating the limitation of only being able to solve quantifiable issues.

Finally, the justification and reasoning process for these AI-generated solutions should be readily understandable to the parties and mediator. The reason why the mediator chooses to ask certain questions or take a particular approach in interacting with the parties is paramount. For example, Solomon's proposal to cut the baby in half was not because he genuinely intended to do so, but because he wanted to gauge the reactions of the women to figure out who the real mother was. In a sense, Solomon was reality-testing their positions to force the women to disclose their underlying interests. Similarly, when the mediator or parties propose solutions, the mediator would guide the parties to understand how their interests can (or cannot) be satisfied by the proposed solution.

To this end, eXplainable AI (XAI) can be used to generate explanations that the mediator and parties can understand. The popularity of XAI has been increasing in a bid to overcome the "black-box" issue of state-of-the-art AI. "Black-box" refers to an AI model where it is not understood how the model derived the outputs from the inputs. With more complex use cases, such as the use of AI in mediation, demanding higher-performing models, there is a trade-off with the explainability of these models. Thus, XAI has been introduced to help end users understand how the model arrived at a result.[27] One possible application of XAI for mediation is showing how the AI prioritised certain interests over others and how the AI arrived at a particular proposed solution. This transparency allows the parties and mediator to assess whether they agree with how the interests have been prioritised, and if they disagree, they can use this information to produce a better solution that fulfils the interests of both parties. However, research of XAI is still relatively nascent and it would still take significant time before commercially available XAI for mediation is produced. Current XAI methods are still highly specific to the type of model and prediction task and require some level of technical awareness that mediators and parties are unlikely to have.[28]

III. Conclusion

In conclusion, state-of-the-art AI can be used in mediation in a human-in-the-loop approach by assisting mediators in relation to their skills of emotional communication and creativity. Deep learning has sufficiently overcome the challenges of unstructured data to allow AI models to better capture the nuances of emotion recognition and communication. Creativity can be algorithmically modelled, with such algorithms optimising for Pareto-optimal outcomes. Hence, AI can be used to help parties and the mediator generate solutions. Even if these solutions are not immediately acceptable to parties, the parties can still use these solutions as a starting point for more acceptable ones. Despite such capabilities, there are still areas of mediation which would be difficult for current AI to learn. These include a general all-in-one system that is able to handle both emotional recognition and communication that account for communication styles across cultures and XAI that is able to explain its analyses in an accessible way to non-technically trained mediators and parties.

https://doi.org/10.1142/9789819801268_bmatter

Endnotes

Chapter 1 Mediation in Addressing Human Rights Violations in Asia

1. DeLaubenfels, C. (2013). The Problem with the duty to adjudicate: How mediations can promote international human rights. *New York University Journal of International Law and Politics*, *46*, 541.
2. Bourdier, F. (2019). From confrontation to mediation: Cambodian farmers expelled by a Vietnamese company. *Journal of Current Southeast Asian Affairs*, *38*(1), 55–76.
3. Maru, V. (2006). Between law and society: Paralegals and the provision of justice services in Sierra Leone and worldwide. *The Yale Journal of International Law*, *31*, 427.
4. Qureshi, W. A. (2017). Water as a human right: A case study of the Pakistan-India water conflict. *Penn State Journal of Law and International Affairs*, *5*, 374.
5. Tiezzi, S. (2014). In South Sudan Conflict, China Tests Its Mediation Skills. *The Diplomat*, *6*.
6. Balch-Lindsay, D., Enterline, A. J., & Joyce, K. A. (2008). Third-party intervention and the civil war process. *Journal of Peace Research*, *45*(3), 345–363.
7. Thio, L. A. (1999). Implementing human rights in ASEAN countries: Promises to keep and miles to go before I sleep. *Yale Human Rights and Development Law Journal*, *2*, 1.
8. Thio, L. A. (2008). Panacea, placebo, or pawn-the teething problems of the human rights commission of Malaysia (Suhakam). *The George Washington International Law Review*, *40*, 1271.
9. Aiman, A. (2019). Govt. to Implement Some Suhakam Recommendations, Says Minister. *Free Malaysia Today*. https://www.freemalaysiatoday.com/category/nation/2019/12/05/govt-to-implement-some-suhakam-recommendations-says-minister/.

10. Crocker, C. A., Hampson, F. O., & Aall, P. R. (2004). *Taming Intractable Conflicts: Mediation in the Hardest Cases*. US Institute of Peace Press.
11. Hernandez, M. B. (2017). *The Philippines' Moro Conflict: The Problems and Prospects in the Quest for a Sustainable Peace*. Doctoral dissertation, Georgetown University.
12. Freeman, M. (2009). *Necessary Evils: Amnesties and the Search for Justice*. Cambridge University Press.
13. Orentlicher, D. F. (1990). Settling accounts: The duty to prosecute human rights violations of a prior regime. *The Yale Law Journal*, *100*, 2537.
14. Paris, R. (2004). *At War's End: Building Peace after Civil Conflict*. Cambridge University Press.
15. Jeffery, R. (2018). Amnesties and Intractable Conflicts: Managed Impunity in The Philippines' Bangsamoro Peace Process. *Journal of Human Rights*, *17*(4), 436–452.
16. Gavilan, J. (2018). 11,103 Victims of Human Rights Violations Under Martial Law to get Compensation. *Rappler*, May 10. https://www.rappler.com/nation/202033-human-rights-victims-claims-board-final-list-eligible-claimants-released/.
17. Deep South Incident Database (2017). Summary of Incidents in Southern Thailand: January 2004–October 2016. *Deep South Watch*.
18. Panjor, F. & Heemmina, A. (2018). Chapter 3: Peace process and transitional justice: The comparative study of Mindanao, Colombia, and Thailand's Deep South. *Asian Affairs: An American Review*, *45*(2), 78–97.
19. Bunyapong, A. (2012). Commission Pays for Monetary Remedy on Kruese-Takbai-Sabayoi Cases, Somchai also Has This Rights. *TCIJ*. http://www.tcijthai.com/news/2012/06/archived/712.
20. Barron, P. (2015). Can Transitional Justice Bring Peace to Thailand's Deep South? *Asia Foundation*. https://asiafoundation.org/2015/02/25/can-transitional-justice-bring-peace-to-thailandsdeep-south.
21. Allan, A., Allan, M. M., Kaminer, D., & Stein, D. J. (2006). Exploration of the association between apology and forgiveness amongst victims of human rights violations. *Behavioral Sciences & the Law*, *24*(1), 87–102.
22. Aroussi, S. & Vandeginste, S. (2013). When interests meet norms: The relevance of human rights for peace and power-sharing. *The International Journal of Human Rights*, *17*(2), 183–203.
23. Burgerman, S. D. (2000). Building the peace by mandating reform: United Nations — mediated human rights agreements in E1 Salvador and Guatemala. *Latin American Perspectives*, *27*(3), 63–87.

24. Cole, G. F., Hanson, R. A., & Silbert, J. E. (1981). Mediation: Is it an effective alternative to adjudication in resolving prisoner complaints. *Judicature, 65*, 481.
25. Peerenboom, R. P. (1993). What's wrong with Chinese Rights: Toward a theory of rights with Chinese characteristics. *Harvard Human Rights Journal, 6*, 29.
26. Sorochinsky, M. (2009). Prosecuting torturers, protecting child molesters: toward a power balance model of criminal process for international human rights law. *Michigan Journal of International Law, 31*, 157.

Chapter 2 The Choice of Law Issue in Article 5(1)(a) Singapore Convention

1. United Nations Convention on International Settlements Agreements resulting from Mediation (adopted 20 December 2018, entered into force 12 September 2020) ("SCM").
2. Schnabel, T. (2019). The Singapore Convention on Mediation: A framework for the cross-border recognition and enforcement of mediated settlements. *Pepperdine Dispute Resolution Law Journal, 19*(1), 1–3.
3. United Nations Convention on the Recognition and Enforcement of Foreign Arbitral Awards (10 June 1958) 330 UNTS 3 ("NYC").
4. SCM (n 1), Arts 3(1)–(2), though note that the SCM does not use the term "recognition", and defines it functionally. See Art 3(2) SCM. For an explanation of why the word "recognition" is not used, see Morris-Sharma, N. Y. (2019). Constructing the Convention on Mediation: The Chairperson's perspective. *SAcLJ, 31*, 500–503.
5. SCM (n 1), Art 5(1)(a).
6. Yokomizo, D. & Mankowski, P. (2022). Article 5: Grounds for refusing to grant relief". In Palao, G. (ed.), *The Singapore Convention on Mediation: A Commentary*. Edward Elgar.
7. Collins, Rule 228(1), 32R-168; see also *Enka v Chubb* [2020] UKSC 38, [95]. The author acknowledges that English common law post-dating 1993 is no longer the law of Singapore, save where affirmed in Singapore by its domestic courts. See s 3(2) Application of English Law Act 1993; see also *Practice Statement: Judicial Precedent* [1994] SLR(R) xcvii. However, English law continues to be of persuasive value. In the absence of any judicial or academic treatment in Singapore law, this author treats English law as an approximation of Singapore law.

8. SCM, Art 5(1)(b)(i).
9. Stephan Wilske, Todd Fox, "Article V(1)(a)" in Wolff, R. ed., *New York Convention: Convention on the Recognition and Enforcement of Foreign Arbitral Awards of 10 June 1958 Commentary* (2012, Beck, Hart Nomos) Art V, [111] ("Wilske and Fox"); *Dallah Real Estate v Ministry of Religious Affairs, Government of Pakistan* [2011] 1 AC 763, [123]–[124].
10. Wilske and Fox (n 10), Art V, [105] See also United National Economic and Social Council, *United Nations Conference on International Commercial Arbitration, Summary Records of the Twenty-Fourth Meeting.* (United Nations, 1958) E/CONF.26/SR.24, 7 (per Prof. Sanders, noting that: "the question of the capacity of the parties, which could be determined only according to the law governing their personal status and not the law applicable to the award").
11. van den Berg, A. J. (1981). *The New York Convention on Arbitration 1958*, 277. Kluwer Law International.
12. Ragno, F. (2020). The incapacity defence under Art V(1)(a) of the New York Convention. In Ferrari, F. & Rosenfeld, F. J. (eds.), *Autonomous Versus Domestic Concepts Under the New York Convention*, 163 Kluwer Arbitration.
13. *Kabab-Ji SAL (Lebanon v Kout Food Group (Kuwait)* (2021) UKSC 48, [30].
14. Ragno (n 12), 165, noting that, "[g]iven the unavailability of an autonomous interpretation of the concept of "personal law" as unequivocally referring to "a one and only law" identifiable *a priori*, the need emerges to supplement the half-way conflict-of-laws rule provided by the first limb of Article V(I)(a) of the New York Convention by relying on the connecting factors that the conflict of laws rules of the forum adopt for the purpose of designating the personal law".
15. UNCITRAL, (2016). *Report of Working Group II (Dispute Settlement) on the Work of its Sixty-Fifth Session,* United Nations A/CN.9/896, [85].
16. Wilske and Fox, 273.
17. UNCITRAL (2015). *International Commercial Conciliation: Enforceability of Settlement Agreements.* Note by the Secretariat, United Nations, A/CN.9/WG.II/WP195, [54].
18. Born, G. (2023). *International Commercial Arbitration* (online edn.) Kluwer Arbitration, para 26(c)(2)(a). For clarity, Born takes the view that the validation principle applies. In this passage, he provides a summation of other leading commentaries in this area.
19. In the absence of other leading works on an autonomous interpretation of incapacity, this chapter will address Ragno's proposed interpretation to avoid creating a straw man.

20. Ragno (n 12), 168–169.
21. *Ibid.*
22. *Ibid.*
23. *Ibid.*
24. Ragno (n 12), 170.
25. *Ibid.*
26. *Ibid.*
27. Nigel Blackaby, K. C., Constantine Partasides, K. C., & Alan Redfern (2023). *Redfern and Hunter on International Arbitration* (7th edn.), Kluwer Arbitration, at para 2.40 et seq.
28. Ragno (n 12), 170: "The preferable view, therefore, is that the drafters of Article V(I)(a) meant just to restate the solution embraced at the time in many civil law legal systems: problems of general capacity and (general) contractual capacity are treated as belonging to the domain of personal law. Conversely, issues of arbitrability ratione personae cannot be considered to fall within the domain of the personal law for the purpose of the first limb of Article V(I)(a) of the New York Convention".
29. Alexander, N., Chong, S., & Giordgadze, V. (2022). *The Singapore Convention on Mediation: A Commentary* (2nd edn.). Kluwer Arbitration, para 5.26.
30. UNCITRAL (2016). *Report of Working Group II (Arbitration and Conciliation) on the Work of Its Sixty-Fourth Session.* United Nations, [152].
31. See, e.g., European Convention on International Commercial Arbitration (adopted 5 May 1960, 7 January 1964) 484 UNTS 349, Arts II(1)–(2); see also *Swiss Private International Law Act*, s 177(2).
32. Alexander, Chong and Giordgadze, para 5.27 et seq.
33. *Id.*; see also the statement of principle in Born, G. (2014). The Law Governing International Arbitration Agreement: An International perspective. *SAcLJ*, *26*, 814, [51]: "if an international arbitration agreement is substantively valid under any of the laws that may potentially be applicable to it, then its validity will be upheld, even if it is not valid under any of the other potentially applicable choices of law".
34. *Hart v O'Connor* [1985] AC 1000, 1027, noting that "[w]here a contracting party suffers from mental incapacity, the contract is voidable for unfairness if it constituted an equitable fraud". See, generally, Phang, A. (1998). Vitiating factors in contract law – The interaction of theory and practice. *SAcLJ*, *10*, 1.
35. *Ibid.*
36. *Gay Choon Ing v Loh Sze Yi Terence Peter* (2009) 2 SLR(R) 332, [46].
37. See A/CN.9/WG.II/WP.195, [55]–[56]: The *travaux preparatoires* reveal that Working Group II had developed a unique proposal for the defences to

recognition and enforcement, but ultimately abandoned it in favour of a draft that adhered more closely to the NYC. See also the Report of the sixty-fourth session, in which Working Group II expressly stated that Art 5(1)(b) SCM was based on Art II(3) NYC.

38. *Ibid.*

Chapter 3 At the Intersection of Justice: Where Victim–Offender Mediations and Singapore's Criminal Justice System Meet

1. Singapore Courts: The Judiciary. (n.d). *Outcomes of a Magistrate's Complaint*. Retrieved from https://www.judiciary.gov.sg/criminal/outcomes-magistrates-complaint.
2. Singapore Courts: The Judiciary. (n.d). *Cases eligible for a Magistrate's Complaint.* Retrieved from https://www.judiciary.gov.sg/criminal/cases-eligible-magistrates-complaint.
3. Singapore Courts: The Judiciary. (n.d). *When a Magistrate's Complaint will end.* Retrieved from https://www.judiciary.gov.sg/criminal/when-magistrates-complaint-will-end.
4. Criminal Procedure Code 2010 (2020 Rev Ed) ("CPC"), ss 11–13.
5. Hoerres, T. (2014). Analysis of the efficacy of criminal court mediation as a tool of restorative justice. *School for International Training Capstone Collection, 281. ("Hoerres")* at 2.
6. Chua, Q. S. C. (2021). Rethinking justice: Introducing victim-offender mediation for sexual offences in Singapore. *National University of Singapore. ("Chua")* at [13].
7. *Ibid at* [13]–[14].
8. Hor, M. (2007). Clashing conceptions of the victim's role in Singapore's criminal process. In Chan, W. C. (ed.) *Support for Victims of Crime in Asia* (1st edn., 207). Singapore: Routledge. *("Hor")* at 209 and 214.
9. *Tay Wee Kiat v PP* [2018] 5 SLR 438 (SGHC) at [7] and [11].
10. *Ibid* at [8]–[10].
11. *Hor,* see note 8 at 213–215.
12. *Chua*, see note 6 generally.
13. This will include, *inter alia*, theft, cheating, hurt, and harassment offences.
14. For example, offences against the state or offences relating to the armed forces.

15. *Chua*, see note 6 at [46].
16. *Ibid.*
17. Koman, R. N. (2016). Balancing the force in criminal mediation. *Beijing Law Review, 7,* 171 (*"Koman"*) at 177.
18. Attorney-General Wong, Y. K. L. (2017, January 14). *Prosecution in the Public Interest.* Retrieved from https://www.agc.gov.sg/docs/default-source/default-document-library/singapore-law-review-annual-lecture-2017---prosecuting-in-the-public-interest.pdf. (*"AG Wong"*) at [9]–[10].
19. *Wu Tze Kok v PP* [2001] 3 SLR(R) 350 (SGHC) at [2].
20. *GCO v PP* at [2019] 3 SLR 1402 (SGHC) [70]–[71].
21. *AG Wong*, see note 18 at [14].
22. *Ibid.*
23. *Ibid.*
24. *Ibid.*
25. *Hor*, see note 8 at 215.
26. *Chua*, see note 6 at [51].
27. Brown, J. G. (1994). The use of mediation to resolve criminal cases: A procedural critique. *Emory Law Journal, 43(4),* 1247. (*"Brown"*) at footnote 148 of 1286.
28. James, D. (2007). Assessing the use (and misuse) of restorative justice in the criminal justice system. In Chan, W. C. (ed.). *Support for Victims of Crime in Asia* (1st edn., 385). Singapore: Routledge. (*"Dignan"*) at 389–390.
29. For example, to contest against one of the elements of the charge, to invoke a defence, to plead for a lower charge, or to defend against a capital charge: See s 227(3) of the CPC.
30. Constitution of the Republic of Singapore (2020 Rev Ed), Art 9(1).
31. Mediation Act 2017 (2020 Rev Ed), ss 9(2)(c), (g)–(j).
32. Rules of Court 2021 (Cap 322)
33. *AG Wong*, see note 18 at [24]; *Hor*, see note 8 at 215.
34. In that the AGC is of the opinion that there is a reasonable prospect for conviction but does not think there is sufficient public interest to prosecute the offender.
35. Stoffels, J. (2020). Victim-offender mediation in the Netherlands. *Tilburg University*. Retrieved from http://arno.uvt.nl/show.cgi?fid=156041. (*"Stoffels"*) at 13–14.
36. *Hoerres*, see note 5 at 29.
37. Parliamentary Debates Singapore: Official Report (Hansard), Vol. 95 (05 March 2021). (Minister for Home Affairs and Minister for Law, K Shanmugam).

38. *Hoerres*, see note 5 at 23.
39. *Brown*, see note 27 at 1291–1301.
40. *Koman*, see note 17 at 177–178.
41. *PP v UI* [2008] 4 SLR(R) 500 (SGCA) at [48].
42. *PP v Shawn Tan Jia Jun* [2022] SGHC 76 at [38]–[39].
43. See also Koh, Y. H. B. (2021). "Paiseh!" – Apologies, restorative justice and criminal mediation in Singapore. In Lee, T. B. J., Lim, M., & Tan, I. (eds.), *Contemporary Issues in Mediation* (6th edn., 105). Singapore: World Scientific. ("*Koh*") at 111–116.
44. *Ng Kean Meng Terence v PP* [2017] 2 SLR 449 (SGCA) at [66].
45. *PP v NF* [2006] 4 SLR(R) 849 (SGHC) at [57].
46. Sentencing Advisory Panel. (2023, August 15). *Guidelines on Reduction in Sentences for Guilty Pleas*. Retrieved from https://www.sentencingpanel.gov.sg/resources/guidelines/guilty-pleas/ at 3 and 4.
47. *Hoerres*, see note 5 at 10.
48. Cf. *Koh*, see note 42 at 113.
49. *Dignan, see* note 28 at 387 (with endnote 4) and 390.
50. *Krishan Chand v PP* [1995] 1 SLR(R) 737 (SGHC) at [13].
51. *Soong Hee Sin v PP* [2001] 1 SLR(R) 475 (SGHC) at [9]–[10].
52. *Chua*, see note 6 at [19].
53. *Ibid.*
54. *Stoffels*, see note 34 at 27.
55. *Ibid.* at 14.
56. *Chua*, see note 6 at [51] and [55].
57. *Ibid.* at [51].
58. Mediation Act 2017 (2020 Rev Ed), s 10.
59. *Stoffels*, see note 34 at 24.
60. *Brown*, see note 27 at 1288–1289.
61. Supreme Court of Judicature Act 1969 (2020 Rev Ed), s 8.
62. *Ibid.*, s 8(5).
63. *Ibid.*, s 8(2A).
64. Uitermak, J. & Mijnarends, I. (2019, October 24). *Mediation in Criminal Cases in the Netherlands*. Retrieved from https://rm.coe.int/mediation-incriminal-cases-oct-2019-oslo-cepej-crystal-scale-of-justic/16809842b4 at slide 17.
65. *Hoerres*, see note 5 at 31.
66. Lim, G. & McFadden, D. (2020). *Mediation in Singapore: A Practical Guide* (3rd edn.). Singapore: Sweet & Maxwell at [14.001]–[14.005].

Chapter 4 Winning Together: Uncovering the Hidden Potential of Game Theory in Mediation

1. Turocy, T. L. & von Stengel, B. (2001). *Game Theory*. CDAM Research Report LSE-CDAM-2001-09, 1–39.
2. *Ibid.*
3. *Ibid.*
4. Camerer, C. F. (1997). Progress in behavioral game theory. *Journal of Economic Perspectives, 11*(4), 167–188. https://doi.org/10.1257/jep.11.4.167.
5. Durlauf, S. N. & Blume, L. E. (2016). *Game Theory*. Springer.
6. Nash, J. (1953). Two-person cooperative games. *Econometrica, 21*(1), 128. https://doi.org/10.2307/1906951.
7. Lima, D. P. (2018). Identifying the game: A game-theoretical approach on the role of the mediator. *Revista Jurídica Da Presidência, 19*(119), 514. https://doi.org/10.20499/2236-3645.rjp2018v19e119-1449.
8. Maschler, M. (2000). Some tips concerning applications of game theory to real problems. In *Game Practice: Contributions from Applied Game Theory*. Organizado Por Fioravante Patrone, Ignacio García-Jurado, E Stef Tijs. Boston, MA: Kluwer Academic.
9. Myerson, R. B. (1991). *Game Theory: Analysis of Conflict*. Cambridge, MA: Harvard University Press.
10. Schelling, T. C. (1980). *The Strategy of Conflict*. Cambridge, MA: Harvard University Press.
11. Bent, D. A. (2001). *Game Theory Explains How Mediation Can Trump Litigation — United States*, June 1. www.mondaq.com. https://www.mondaq.com/unitedstates/litigation-mediation-arbitration/11840/game-theory-explains-how-mediation-can-trump-litigation.
12. Maschler, M. *Op. cit.*
13. Chatterjee, K. & Samuelson, W. (eds.) (2014). *Game Theory and Business Applications: International Series in Operations Research & Management Science*, Vol. 194 (2nd edn.). London: Springer.
14. Hofstede, G. (2011). Dimensionalizing Cultures: The Hofstede Model in Context. *Online Readings in Psychology and Culture*, 2(1).
15. Tversky, A. & Thaler, R. H. (1990). Anomalies: Preference reversals. *Journal of Economic Perspectives*, *4*(2), 201–211. https://doi.org/10.1257/jep.4.2.201.
16. Tversky, A. & Kahneman, D. (1981). The framing of decisions and the psychology of choice. *Science*, *211*(4481), 453–458. https://doi.org/10.1126/science.7455683.

17. Bond, K. (2021). Riskin's Grid: Do You Need a Facilitator or an Evaluator? *JD Supra*, June 24. https://www.jdsupra.com/legalnews/riskin-s-grid-do-you-need-a-facilitator-4319757/.

Chapter 5 The Role of Negative Emotions in Mediation

1. Kelly, E. J. & Kaminskienė, N. (2016, July 5). Importance of emotional intelligence in negotiation and mediation. *International Comparative Jurisprudence*, 56. Retrieved April 2, 2023, from https://www.sciencedirect.com/science/article/pii/S2351667416300130.
2. Fisher, R. & Shapiro, D. (2006). *Beyond Reason: Using Emotions as You Negotiate*. Random House Business Books, New York, NY, p. 4.
3. *Ibid.*
4. Kelly & Kaminskienė (2016), *Op. cit.*, 55.
5. *Ibid.*, 56.
6. *Ibid.*
7. *Ibid.*, 57.
8. Fisher & Shapiro (2006), *Op. cit.*, p. 146.
9. Kahneman, D. & Thaler, R. H. (2006). Anomalies: Utility maximization and experienced utility. *Journal of Economic Perspectives*, *20*(1), 221–234, 224. https://doi.org/10.2139/ssrn.870494.
10. *Ibid.*, 225.
11. *Ibid.*, 227.
12. *Ibid.*
13. Kelly & Kaminskienė (2016), *Op. cit.*, 55.
14. *Ibid.*, 57.
15. *Ibid.*
16. Mueller, J. S. & Curhan, J. R. (2006). Emotional intelligence and counterpart mood induction in a negotiation. *International Journal of Conflict Management*, *17*(2), 110–128. https://doi.org/10.1108/10444060610736602.
17. Kelly & Kaminskienė (2016), *Op. cit.*, 57.
18. *Ibid.*
19. Schreier, L. S. (2002). Emotional intelligence and mediation training. *Conflict Resolution Quarterly*, *20*(1), 99–119, 110. https://doi.org/10.1002/crq.13.
20. *Ibid.*, 103.
21. Kelly & Kaminskienė (2016), *Op. cit.*, 57.

22. *Ibid.*
23. *Ibid.*
24. *Ibid.*
25. Fisher & Shapiro (2006), *Op. cit.*, pp. 28–29.
26. Kelly & Kaminskienė (2016), *Op. cit.*, 58.
27. Fisher & Shapiro (2006), *Op. cit.*, p. 12.
28. *Ibid.*, 15–17.
29. *Ibid.*, 18.
30. *Ibid.*, 17.
31. *Ibid.*, 153.
32. Williams, K. E. & Hinshaw, A. (2018). Outbursts: An evolutionary approach to emotions in the mediation context. *Negotiation Journal*, *34*(2), 165–186, 173. https://doi.org/10.1111/nejo.12222.
33. Fisher & Shapiro (2006), *Op. cit.*, p. 17.
34. Williams & Hinshaw (2018), *Op. cit.*, 174.
35. Fisher & Shapiro (2006), *Op. cit.*, p. 57.
36. *Ibid.*, p. 17.
37. Kelly & Kaminskienė (2016), *Op. cit.*, 58.
38. Fisher & Shapiro (2006), *Op. cit.*, p. 17.
39. *Ibid.*, p. 153.
40. Lerner, J. S., Li, Y., Valdesolo, P., & Kassam, K. S. (2015). Emotion and decision making. *Annual Review of Psychology*, *66*(1), 799–823, 811. https://doi.org/10.1146/annurev-psych-010213-115043.
41. Fisher & Shapiro (2006), *Op. cit.*, p. 149.
42. Lerner *et al.* (2015), *Op. cit.*, 810.
43. *Ibid.*
44. *Ibid.*
45. *Ibid.*
46. *Ibid.*
47. Kopelman, S., Rosette, A. S., & Thompson, L. (2006). The three faces of eve: Strategic displays of positive, negative, and neutral emotions in negotiations. *Organizational Behavior and Human Decision Processes*, *99*(1), 81–101, 97. https://doi.org/10.1016/j.obhdp.2005.08.003.
48. Jamieson, J. P., Mendes, W. B., & Nock, M. K. (2013). Improving acute stress responses. *Current Directions in Psychological Science*, *22*(1), 51–56, 1. https://doi.org/10.1177/0963721412461500.
49. Fisher & Shapiro (2006), *Op. cit.*, p. 149.
50. Lerner *et al.* (2015), *Op. cit.*, 812.

51. Jamieson *et al.* (2013), *Op. cit.*, 2.
52. *Ibid.*, 3.
53. Zhan, J., Wu, X., Fan, J., Guo, J., Zhou, J., Ren, J., Liu, C., & Luo, J. (2017). Regulating anger under stress via cognitive reappraisal and sadness. *Frontiers in Psychology*, *8*, 1. https://doi.org/10.3389/fpsyg.2017.01372.
54. *Ibid.*
55. Slovic, P., Finucane, M. L., Peters, E., & MacGregor, D. G. (2004). Risk as analysis and risk as feelings: Some thoughts about affect, reason, risk, and rationality. *Risk Analysis*, *24*(2), 311–322, 311. https://doi.org/10.1111/j.0272-4332.2004.00433.x.
56. Slovic *et al.* (2004), *Op. cit.*, 319.
57. *Ibid.*, 316.
58. *Ibid.*, 316–317.
59. *Ibid.*, 317.
60. *Ibid.*, 315.
61. *Ibid.*
62. *Ibid.*

Chapter 6 Investigating Neighbour Disputes and Mediation in Singapore through Behavioural Economics to Foster Stronger Communities

1. *HDB* (n.d.). Public Housing — A Singapore Icon — Housing & Development Board (HDB). https://www.hdb.gov.sg/about-us/our-role/public-housing-a-singapore-icon.
2. Koh, W. T. (2023). Officers can Enter Homes in Neighbour Dispute Cases under Proposed Changes to Framework. *CNA*, May 10. https://www.channelnewsasia.com/singapore/proposed-enhancements-neighbours-community-dispute-management-framework-public-consultation-3477651.
3. *Insight MinLaw* (2022). Getting to the Heart of Community Conflicts. Ministry of Law, March 18. https://insight.mlaw.gov.sg/articles/our-people/2022-03-18-getting-to-the-heart-of-community-conflicts/.
4. Liew, I. (2024). Tackling Noisy Neighbours, Elder-Friendly Flat Features among Highlights of MND Budget Debate. *The Straits Times*, March 5. https://www.straitstimes.com/singapore/politics/tackling-noisy-neighbours-elder-friendly-flat-features-among-highlights-from-mnd-budget-debate.
5. *Insight MinLaw*. *Op. cit.*

6. Managing Neighbour Disputes (n.d.). *Housing & Development Board*. https://www.hdb.gov.sg/residential/living-in-an-hdb-flat/my-neighbourhood/managing-neighbour-disputes.
7. Rodman, L. & Gorbatov, S. (2019). For Impactful Feedback, Context and Tone are Required. *Duke Corporate Education*, March 6. https://www.dukece.com/insights/fo-impactful-feedback-context-and-tone-are-required/.
8. Hardavella, G., Aamli-Gaagnat, A., Saad, N., Rousalova, I., & Sreter, K. B. (2017). How to give and receive feedback effectively. *Breathe*, *13*(4), 327–333. https://doi.org/10.1183/20734735.009917.
9. The Mediation Process (n.d.). *Community Mediation Centre*. https://cmc.mlaw.gov.sg/apply-for-mediation/the-mediation-process/.
10. Chen, J. (2021). What is Homo Economicus? Definition, Meaning, and Origins. *Investopedia*, July 31. https://www.investopedia.com/terms/h/homoeconomicus.asp.
11. Fisher, R. & Ury, W. (1991). *Getting to Yes: Negotiating Agreement Without Giving In* (2nd edn.). Houghton Mifflin.
12. Kahneman, D., Knetsch, J. L., & Thaler, R. H. (1991). Anomalies: The endowment effect, loss aversion, and status quo bias. *Journal of Economic Perspectives*, *5*(1), 193–206. https://doi.org/10.1257/jep.5.1.193.
13. Kahneman, D. & Tversky, A. (1979). Prospect theory: An analysis of decision under risk. *Econometrica*, *47*(2), 263–292. https://doi.org/10.2307/1914185.
14. Kahneman, D. (2011). *Thinking, Fast and Slow*. Farrar, Straus and Giroux.
15. *Ibid*.
16. *Ibid*.
17. *Ibid*.
18. Ko, H. (2009). On the role of a mediator: A behavioural law and economics perspective. *Asia Pacific Law Review*, *17*(Supp. 1), 195–204. https://doi.org/10.1080/10192557.2009.11788218.
19. Ross, L. & Ward, A. (1995). Psychological barriers to dispute resolution. *Advances in Experimental Social Psychology*, *27*, 255–304. https://doi.org/10.1016/s0065-2601(08)60407-4.
20. Ross, L. & Stillinger, C. (1991). Barriers to conflict resolution. *Negotiation Journal*, *7*(4), 389–404. https://doi.org/10.1007/bf01000332.
21. Ko, H. *Op. cit*.
22. Ross, L. & Ward, A. *Op. cit*.
23. Ross, L. & Center, S. (1993). *Reactive Devaluation in Negotiation and Conflict Resolution*. Stanford Center On Conflict and Negotiation, Stanford University.

24. Ross, L. & Ward, A. *Op. cit.*
25. *Ibid.*
26. *Ibid.*
27. Koh, W. T. *Op. cit.*
28. Sharot, T. (2011). The optimism bias. *Current Biology*, *21*(23), R941–R945. https://doi.org/10.1016/j.cub.2011.10.030.
29. Dunning, D., Griffin, D. W., Milojkovic, J. D., & Ross, L. (1990). The overconfidence effect in social prediction. *Journal of Personality and Social Psychology*, *58*(4), 568–581. https://doi.org/10.1037/0022-3514.58.4.568.
30. Bazerman, M. H. (1990). *Judgment in Managerial Decision Making* (2nd edn.). John Wiley and Sons.
31. Ross, L. & Ward, A. *Op. cit.*
32. Tversky, A. & Kahneman, D. (1973). Availability: A heuristic for judging frequency and probability. *Cognitive Psychology*, *5*(2), 207–232. https://www.sciencedirect.com/science/article/abs/pii/0010028573900339.
33. Babcock, L. & Loewenstein, G. (1997). Explaining bargaining impasse: The role of self-serving biases. *Journal of Economic Perspectives*, *11*(1), 109–126. https://doi.org/10.1257/jep.11.1.109.
34. Ross, L. & Ward, A. *Op. cit.*
35. The Mediation Process (n.d.). *Op. cit.*
36. Ross, L. & Ward, A. *Op. cit.*
37. Rubin, J. Z. (1994). Models of conflict management. *Journal of Social Issues*, *50*(1), 33–45. https://doi.org/10.1111/j.1540-4560.1994.tb02396.x.
38. Cultural Atlas Editors (2015). Singaporean Culture — Core Concepts. *Cultural Atlas*. https://culturalatlas.sbs.com.au/singaporean-culture/singaporean-culture-core-concepts.
39. Ko, H. *Op. cit.*
40. Fairhurst, G. T. & Sarr, R. A. (1996). *The Art of Framing: Managing the Language of Leadership*. Jossey-Bass Publishers.
41. Ross, L. & Ward, A. *Op. cit.*
42. *Ibid.*
43. *Ibid.*
44. Liberman, V., Samuels, S. M., & Ross, L. (2004). The name of the game: Predictive power of reputations versus situational labels in determining prisoner's dilemma game moves. *Personality and Social Psychology Bulletin*, *30*(9), 1175–1185. https://doi.org/10.1177/0146167204264004.
45. Ross, L. & Ward, A. *Op. cit.*
46. The Mediation Process (n.d.). *Op. cit.*

Chapter 7 Learning through Competing: The Pedagogical Value of Mediation Competitions in Mediation Education

1. For instance, see National University of Singapore's course outline for its Mediation Workshop: https://law1a.nus.edu.sg/student_matters/course_listing/docs/LL4044V-Mediation%20Workshop%20(2220).pdf.
2. Smolinski, R. & Kesting, P. (2013). World championship in negotiation? The role of competitions in negotiation pedagogy. *Negotiation Journal*, *29*(3), 355–369 at 356.
3. Druckman, D. & Ebner, N. (2013). Games, claims, and new frames: Rethinking the use of simulation in negotiation education. *Negotiation Journal*, *29*(1), 61–92 at 63.
4. *Druckman* at 64.
5. *Ibid.*
6. *Smolinski* at 356.
7. *Smolinski* at 361.
8. Cojic, S. (2022, March 1). *FDI Mediation Moot: Calling All Professionals!*. International Mediation Institute. https://imimediation.org/2022/03/01/fdi-mediation-moot-calling-all-professionals/ (accessed October 20, 2024).
9. *Smolinski* at 360.
10. Avruch, K. (2000). Culture and negotiation pedagogy. *Negotiation Journal*, *16*(4), 339 at 340–341.
11. Bond, G. (2013). Mediation and culture: The example of the ICC International Commercial Mediation Competition. *Negotiation Journal*, *29*(3), 315–328 ("Bond") at 324.
12. *Smolinski* at 361.
13. *Ibid.*
14. *Smolinski* at 362.
15. *Bond* at 319.
16. *Bond* at 322.
17. *Bond* at 320.
18. *Singapore Mediation Centre* (2022). SMC Training, December 23. https://www.mediation.com.sg/smc-training (accessed February 27, 2023).
19. *Bond* at 323.
20. *Smolinski* at 362.
21. Parks, G. (2010). Where do we belong? New mediators' roles in current practice. *Student Lawyer*, *38*, 16.

22. *Ibid.*
23. *Parks* at 17.
24. *NUS Law* (2021). NUS Law Alumni Appointed Young IP Mediators in 2021 by IPOS, September 30. https://law.nus.edu.sg/media/nus-law-alumni-appointed-young-ip-mediators-in-2021-by-ipos/ (accessed February 27, 2023).

Chapter 8 Contemporary View on the Legislative Improvement of Mediation and Mediation Technologies in Socially Relevant Areas in Russia

1. Welsh, N. A. (2001). The thinning vision of self-determination in court-connected mediation: The inevitable price of institutionalization? *Harvard Negotiation Law Review*, *6*, 1–96.
2. Federal Law No. 193-FZ of July 27, 2010. On the alternative procedure of settlement of disputes with the participation of a mediator (mediation procedure). https://www.consultant.ru/document/cons_doc_LAW_103038/?ysclid=li615ekpu5933715251.

Chapter 9 Resolving Drama with a Trauma-informed Approach in Family Mediation

1. Collins Dictionary. (n.d.). *Collins Dictionary*. Retrieved from Drama. https://www.collinsdictionary.com/dictionary/english/drama#:~:text=a%20situation%20or%20sequence%20of,Collins%20English%20Dictionary.
2. U.S. Department of Justice Office of Justice Programs Bureau of Justice Statistics. (2003–2012). *Special Report Nonfatal Domestic Violence, 2003–2012*. Retrieved from https://bjs.ojp.gov/content/pub/pdf/ndv0312.pdf.
3. GLG Legal Springfield. (n.d.). *The Difference between Family Violence and Domestic Abuse — What to Know*. Retrieved from GLG Legal Springfield. https://www.springfieldlegals.com.au/difference-family-violence-and-domestic-abuse/.
4. United Nations. (n.d.). *Examining Domestic Violence around the World: The Cost of Doing Nothing*. Retrieved from United Nations. https://www.un.org/en/academic-impact/examining-domestic-violence-around-world-cost-doing-nothing.

5. Shafeeq, S. (2023, May 9). Proposed Changes to Boost Protection for Family Violence Victims, Rehab for Abusers. Retrieved from *The Straits Times*. https://www.straitstimes.com/singapore/politics/proposed-changes-to-boost-protection-for-family-violence-victims-rehab-for-abusers.
6. American Psychological Association. (n.d.). *Trauma*. Retrieved from American Psychological Association: https://www.apa.org/topics/trauma.
7. Evans, O. G. (2023, May 15). *Fight, Flight, Freeze, or Fawn: How We Respond to Threats*. Retrieved from SimplyPsychology. https://www.simplypsychology.org/fight-flight-freeze-fawn.html.
8. Human Relations Institute & Clinics. (n.d.). *Trauma Response (The 4 F's – Fight, Flight, Freeze, and Fawn)*. Retrieved from Human Relations Institute & Clinics. https://www.hricdubai.com/trauma-response-the-4fs/#:~:text=The%20responses%20are%20usually%20referred,quickly%20to%20life%2Dthreatening%20situations.
9. University at Buffalo. (n.d.). *What is Trauma-Informed Care?* Retrieved from University at Buffalo Buffalo Center for Social Research. https://socialwork.buffalo.edu/social-research/institutes-centers/institute-on-trauma-and-trauma-informed-care/what-is-trauma-informed-care.html.
10. *Ibid.*
11. Naybour, P. (2021, January 13). *ZOPA, BATNA and Win-Win in Negotiation*. Retrieved from Parallel Project Training. https://www.parallelprojecttraining.com/blog/zopa-batna-and-win-win-in-negotiation/#:~:text=These%20are%20Zone%20of%20Possible,BATNA)%20and%20Win%2DWin.
12. Social Care Institute for Excellence. (n.d.). *Strengths-Based Approaches*. Retrieved from Social Care Institute for Excellence. https://www.scie.org.uk/strengths-based-approaches#:~:text=Strengths%2Dbased%20(or%20asset%2D,individual%20to%20promote%20their%20wellbeing.
13. SG Courts. (n.d.). *Judiciary*. Retrieved from Therapeutic justice in the Family Justice Courts. https://www.judiciary.gov.sg/who-we-are/therapeutic-justice.
14. British Medical Association. (2022, January 17). *British Medical Association*. Retrieved from Vicarious trauma: Signs and strategies for coping. https://www.bma.org.uk/advice-and-support/your-wellbeing/vicarious-trauma/vicarious-trauma-signs-and-strategies-for-coping.
15. Goh, Y. H. (2023, May 03). From 'Nobody Cares' to 'I'm Not Alone': Male Victims of Family Violence Find Support in New Scheme. Retrieved from *The Straits Times*. https://www.straitstimes.com/singapore/from-nobody-cares-to-i-m-not-alone-male-victims-of-family-violence-find-support-in-new-scheme.

Chapter 10 How can Artificial Intelligence Assist Mediators: A Technical Analysis

1. Del Duca, L. F., Rule, C., & Rimpfel, K. (2014). eBay's De Facto low value high volume resolution process: Lessons and best practices for ODR systems designers. *Arbitration Law Review*, *6*(1), 204–219.
2. Personal Data Protection Commission (PDPC). (2020). *Model AI Governance Framework Second Edition*. https://www.pdpc.gov.sg/-/media/files/pdpc/pdf-files/resource-for-organisation/ai/sgmodelaigovframework2.pdf.
3. Anantrasirichai, N., & Bull, D. (2021). Artificial intelligence in the creative industries: a review. In *Artificial Intelligence Review* (Vol. 55, No. 1, pp. 589–656). Springer Science and Business Media LLC. https://doi.org/10.1007/s10462-021-10039-7.
4. Kasap, G. H. (2021). Can artificial intelligence ("AI") replace human arbitrators? Technological concerns and legal implications. *Journal of Dispute Resolution*, *2021*(2), 209.
5. Riskin, L. L. (1996). Understanding mediators' orientations, strategies, and techniques: A grid for the perplexed. *Harvard Negotiation Law Review, 1*, 7, 24.
6. Soh, J. (2018, March 22). Document management systems. *Singapore Academy of Law*. https://www.sal.org.sg/Resources-Tools/Legal-Technology-Vision/Software/Document-Management-Systems.
7. Kelly, E. J. & Kaminskienė, N. (2016). Importance of emotional intelligence in negotiation and mediation. *International Comparative Jurisprudence, 2*(1), 55–60.
8. Fisher, R., Ury, W. L., & Patton, B. (2011). *Getting to Yes: Negotiating Agreement without Giving In*. Penguin, New York.
9. Ahmed, N., Al Aghbari, Z., & Girija, S. (2023). A systematic survey on multimodal emotion recognition using learning algorithms. *Intelligent Systems with Applications, 17*, 200171.
10. Chawla, K., Clever, R., Ramirez, J., Lucas, G., & Gratch, J. (2021, September). Towards emotion-aware agents for negotiation dialogues. In *2021 9th International Conference on Affective Computing and Intelligent Interaction (ACII)* (pp. 1–8). IEEE.
11. Knapp, M. L., Hall, J. A., & Horgan, T. G. (2013). *Nonverbal Communication in Human Interaction*. Cengage Learning, Belmont, CA.
12. Fisher *et al.* (2011), *Op. cit.*
13. Kelly & Kaminskiene (2016), *Op. cit.*

14. Goswamy, T., Singh, I., Barkati, A., & Modi, A. (2020, December). Adapting a language model for controlled affective text generation. In *Proceedings of the 28th International Conference on Computational Linguistics* (pp. 2787–2801).
15. Alessa, H. (2022). The role of artificial intelligence in online dispute resolution: A brief and critical overview. *Information & Communications Technology Law, 31*(3), 319–342.
16. Snitker, T. V. (2010). The impact of culture on user research. In *Handbook of Global User Research* (pp. 257–277). Morgan Kaufmann, Burlington, USA.
17. Kelly & Kaminskiene (2016), *Op. cit.*
18. Alessa (2022), *Op. cit.*
19. Fisher *et al.* (2011), *Op. cit.*
20. Abramson, H. (2005). Problem-solving advocacy in mediations: A model of client representation. *Harvard Negotiation Law Review, 10*, 103.
21. Silver, D., Huang, A., Maddison, C. J., Guez, A., Sifre, L., Van Den Driessche, G., ... & Hassabis, D. (2016). Mastering the game of Go with deep neural networks and tree search. *Nature, 529*(7587), 484–489.
22. Lodder, A. R. & Zelznikow, J. (2005). Developing an online dispute resolution environment: Dialogue tools and negotiation support systems in a three-step model. *Harvard Negotiation Law Review, 10*, 287.
23. Li, M., Vo, Q. B., & Kowalczyk, R. (2009, May). Searching for fair joint gains in agent-based negotiation. In *Proceedings of The 8th International Conference on Autonomous Agents and Multiagent Systems-Volume 2* (pp. 1049–1056).
24. Dai, T., Sycara, K., & Zheng, R. (2021). Agent Reasoning in AI-Powered Negotiation. In *Handbook of Group Decision and Negotiation* (pp. 1187–1211). Springer International Publishing. https://doi.org/10.1007/978-3-030-49629-6_26.
25. Larson, D. A. (2010). Brother, can you spare a dime-technology can reduce dispute resolution costs when times are tough and improve outcomes. *Nevada Law Journal, 11*, 523.
26. *English Standard Version Bible*. (2016). Crossway Bibles. *1 Kings, 3*, 16–28 (Original work published in 2001).
27. Danilevsky, M., Qian, K., Aharonov, R., Katsis, Y., Kawas, B., & Sen, P. (2020). A survey of the state of explainable AI for natural language processing. *arXiv preprint* arXiv:2010.00711.
28. Zini, J. E. & Awad, M. (2022). On the explainability of natural language processing deep models. *ACM Computing Surveys, 55*(5), 1–31.

https://doi.org/10.1142/9789819801268_bmatter

Index

www.ingramcontent.com/pod-product-compliance
Lightning Source LLC
Chambersburg PA
CBHW060645121126
54737CB00004B/466
9789819801251